Travellii

The "must have" guide to a
safe and healthy journey.

Dr Deborah Mills MBBS

November 2000

© Deborah Mills

First Edition	May 1989
Second Edition	November 1990
Third Edition	April 1992
Fourth Edition	July 1994
Fifth Edition	August 1995
Sixth Edition	July 1996
Seventh Edition	October 1997
Eighth Edition	July 1999
Ninth Edition	November 2000

Published by Dr Deborah Mills
PO Box 375 Albion 4010 Brisbane Australia
Phone 0408 199 166 Fax 61 7 3256 1257
Website: www.travellingwell.com.au
Email;   dmills@travellingwell.com.au

Over 62,000 copies in print
Translated into Braille and Vietnamese
Also by the same author 'Travelling Well Fun Book'

All comments or suggestions for improvements to future editions will be gratefully received. Please send to above address.

Every effort has been made to ensure the information in this book is up to date at the time of printing, however no responsibility will be taken for the results of any actions taken on the basis of information in this work, nor for any errors or omissions. The traveller is strongly urged to see a doctor experienced in travel medicine prior to departure.

National Library of Australia Cataloguing-in-Publication entry:

Mills, D.J.
    Travelling well

    (Rev. ed.)
    Includes index.
    ISBN 0 9577179 1 1

    1. Travel - Health Aspects. I. Title

613.68

TRAVELLING WELL

'There are three things I wouldn't dream of leaving Australia without – a passport, a sarong and a copy of **Travelling Well** *tucked into my first aid kit. Its a hell of a lot cheaper than carting a real-live physician around the world with you!.. (and the crew are always borrowing it to diagnose themselves on the road.) It's a gem.'*
Sorrel Wilby — World traveller and presenter on Getaway

'Travelling Well is a great travel companion. It is packed full of information and is so easy to refer to. Everything you may need to find out about, from "Accidents" to "Yellow Fever". It is a must read before, during and after your travel adventures.'
Grant Kenny — Phenomenal athlete and world traveller

'The information in this book, and the medicines that go with it, are a very valuable thing when in a country where the hospitals can make you sicker than you already are. Thank you very much for your help so far in my travels.'
Chris Barnes — Ongoing traveller – Central and South America

'The eternal dilemma of which tablet, when and why! This book is an invaluable resource in answering this question and many more when medical assistance may be unavailable or just plain dodgy! Keep it stashed somewhere amongst all those other essentials.'
Kathryn Fulton. — Ongoing traveller – Middle East and Africa

'Thank you **Travelling Well** *for 18 months of guidance in India, Nepal, Africa and Madagascar. You gave us (and all those who borrowed you) peace of mind when we were isolated and proved a true friend in times of need with diarrhoea and infection! Thanks to you we fulfilled our dream of marriage on the summit of Mt Kilimanjaro in excellent shape, as we watched others battling with the altitude or even being forced to turn back. Sadly, we also heard of the preventable (?) death of a trekker from acute mountain sickness that very week. Thank you for keeping us safe and for being written in such a user friendly, easy to understand style.'*
Lucinda and Ed Shelton — Safely returned to Australia

'Travelling Well is a precious publication. This book provides all the necessary information on the prevention of travel related sickness. I wish this book had been available while I was an airline manager based in Tokyo. It could have helped many Japanese travellers who have had to suffer unnecessarily during or upon their return from their holiday.'
Yukiko White — Former Air Nuigini Regional Manager for South East Asia and Micronesia

What other doctors say about
TRAVELLING WELL

'Full of sensble, easy to follow advice......the section "If You Get Sick" is particularly helpful to travellers'
Dr Gil Lea, MBBS (Lon)
Medical Consultant in Travel Health, Trailfinders Travel Clinic, London —UK

*'Travel Medicine is a highly specialised area that requires dedication and concerted attention. Dr Deb Mills is a recognised pioneer and leader in this field in Australia and neighbouring regions. Information gleaned from years of experience has been condensed into **Travelling Well**, a book that presents, in succinct and straightforward language, all the important, practical health information that any prospective traveller might need, before, during or after their trip.'*
Dr Paul Prociv, MBBS, PhD, FRACP, FRCPA
Associate Professor, Dept of Microbiology & Parasitology, UQ — Australia

*'**Travelling Well** contains the essential information that travellers need to protect their health overseas. The feedback from our patients is that this book is extremely useful and worthy of a place in their luggage.'*
Dr Norman Hohl, MBBS, DTM&H, FAFPHM
Medical Director, The Travel Doctor-TMVC, Gold Coast—Australia

*'Clear, concise, practical and without doubt the most user-friendly travel health book available. This book is essential reading for all travellers. Prevention and treatment of common travellers' health problems are covered in an easy to read and understand format. I feel secure that when my clients travel with a copy of **Travelling Well** they have an excellent tool to help them on their way to having a great trip. A true don't-leave-home-without-it item.'*
Dr Trish Batchelor, MBBS
Medical Director, The Travel Doctor-TMVC — New Zealand

*'Travel medicine is more than a few jabs and tablets for diarrhoea. Information on how to stay healthy while travelling and how to manage minor medical problems efficiently and effectively is essential. **Travelling Well** is written by one of the Australia's most experienced travel medicine practitioners and will make an excellent companion in your travels.'*
Dr Bob Kass, MBBS MRCP MScMCH DCH FAFPHM
International Public Health Consultant, The Travel Doctor-TMVC —Australia

ACKNOWLEDGMENTS

This book is gratefully dedicated to:

- My husband Robert, my mum, my siblings Liane and Roy, for listening to me talk about this book so much and for their unceasing encouragement and moral support, (and minding the kids while I worked on it).
- Laura and Chrissy for teaching me all those things about children that you cannot learn from books.
- Every one of my travelling patients for their support, stories and helpful suggestions.
- All those travellers who sent in photos of their trips – I wish we had more space on the cover to show them off.
- TMVC for their help and support.
- My Macintosh computer, and my friend Bill who introduced me to macs.
- My dentist, Dr Dennis Krafft for assistance with dental information
- Dr Julie Lauman for her two first aid drawings.
- Thanks to Pam Nimitz DeMaris, USA, International Security Expert for her input on the personal security section.
- Most of all to my wonderful father, whose memory will always give me strength and inspiration.

CONTENTS

Page

Acknowledgements..*(v)*

Foreword — by Major General John Pearn..........................1
How to use this book 3
Introduction...5

BEFORE YOU GO 6

Vaccinations..8
Malaria Prevention....................................15
Travellers Medical Kit................................23
Pre - travel Checkups................................29
Fitness Training...33
Jetlag Prevention......................................34
Packing...35

WHILE YOU ARE AWAY!.......................37

During the Flight..38
Adapting to New Time Zones.....................40
Gastro Prevention.....................................42
Safe Drinking Water..................................44
Clues to pick a Safe Restaurant................46
Accidents..47
Sex and Disease.......................................51
Mind Altering Drugs..................................52
Insect Bites...53
Rabies...54
Worms and Parasites................................55
Hot Climates...56
Cold Climates...58
Women Travellers......................................59
Personal Security......................................62
Travelling with Children.............................63
High Altitude Travellers.............................64
Going to the snow.....................................67
Scuba Divers...69
Motion sickness..70
Culture Shock...72

IF YOU GET SICK...75

Travellers First Aid..76
Finding Doctors overseas.................................76
8 keys for treating any illness...........................77
Side effects of medication.................................78
Fevers..79
Gut problems in travellers................................83
Coughs, Colds, Chest infections......................93
Skin Damage..94
Hangovers..104
Hot Climate Problems......................................104
Cold Climate Problems.....................................105
Eyes...106
Ears...107
Teeth and Mouth..108
Muscles and Joints...109
Bladder and Kidneys..110
Thrush...111
Emergency contraception.................................111
General emergencies..113
Children Travellers' First Aid............................115
Drug Reference Table.......................................116

A FEW DETAILS...124

WHEN YOU GET HOME 148

INDEX 152

FOREWORD

International travel and widespread national excursions have become the norm. Almost three million Australians travel overseas each year; and our national prosperity depends significantly on the income derived from more than nine million travellers coming to Australia annually.

Each leave the secure base of their own home and community; and enjoy the adventures of new experiences. Every new geographic region brings with it the potential for new illnesses and injuries; and those who extend the long "travellers umbilical cord" away from their own families, doctors and personal health care systems venture into unfamiliar territory.

Mostly being a tourist or business traveller poses no health problems. But much can be done to prevent illness or injury when one is away from one's own familiar places and this book will help the traveller become a "street-wise tourist".

Extended national and international travel is now a normal way of life for almost everybody in society. This book will help one to experience new places and meet new people without such enjoyment being spoilt by illness or disease.

Major General John Pearn
The Surgeon General,
Australian Defence Force.

HOW TO USE THIS BOOK

No book can tell you exactly what you need for any particular country or trip.

Information changes all the time, and requirements vary depending on your past health, what vaccines you have had before, what you will be doing while you are away, and what part of a particular country you are visiting. You need to consult a doctor experienced in Travel Medicine to get up-to-date information about the exact requirements for your particular trip.

This book will teach you the background information about how to stay healthy while travelling. It is designed to be used in conjunction with a doctor's consultation.

Travelling Well is divided into sections for easy reference.

Initially you may read the section *Before You Go* which deals with vaccinations, malaria prevention, medical kits and checkups.

Once you are away, perhaps on the plane, you need to thoroughly familiarise yourself with the hints on how to stay healthy *While You Are Away.*

Hopefully you will not need it, but the section on *If You Get Sick* will tell you all about travellers' first aid. Generic drug names are in lower case where possible.

A Few Details is for those readers interested in finding out more information about the various diseases.

When You Get Home gives important information on post travel precautions and checkups.

The *Index* will help you locate information about particular diseases, drugs etc.

*'Of the gladdest moments in human life...
is the departure on a distant journey
into unknown lands'*

*Sir Richard Burton
late 19th century explorer*

INTRODUCTION

..So you are going travelling!! There is much to be done - organising tickets, visas, passports, traveller's cheques - and organising your *good health*. We all want to make the most of every minute of our trip. Travel is about new experiences, but sickness or accidents are experiences we can all do without!

In March 1991, a young man from Brisbane died of malaria contracted in Thailand. In June 1996, a 32-year-old American tourist was bitten by a street dog she stopped to pat in Kathmandu. Two months later she died of rabies. These two examples of *preventable* tragedies dramatically highlight the vital importance of sufficient pre-travel preparation. There are many diseases travellers are not familiar with. Many hazards can be avoided if you know how, or minimised with rapid and appropriate treatment.

Pre travel preparation is the key!

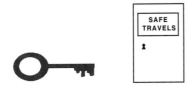

People travel for different reasons, and in different degrees of style; backpackers, businessmen, shoppers, missionaries, ministers of government, honeymooners, to visit family and friends. No matter what your reason to travel, this book is designed to assist you, dear reader, to minimise the health risks of your trip - the easy way - without pain and suffering. The goal is to be careful without being paranoid. Reading this book is the first step towards preparing yourself for a healthy trip - towards 'Travelling Well'.

What if 'nothing is compulsory' for my trip?

You may still be *highly recommended* to have certain vaccinations, medications or advice for your trip. A traveller's medical kit can be useful no matter where you go. 'Compulsory' requirements are made to protect the local inhabitants, *not the visitor*. Developing countries usually pose greater risks, yet even travellers to industrialised countries like Europe, UK, USA may need something. Can you remember when you had your last tetanus and diphtheria booster? You need them at least every ten years.

BEFORE YOU GO

**Most travellers need to
seek medical advice
8 weeks
before departure.**

**For those going to live
or work overseas,
you need to seek advice
6 months
prior to departure.**

**For those leaving
at short notice,
it is never too late
to seek advice.**

What Vaccines Do I Need?

The following is a rough guide only. No book can tell you exactly what you need because recommendations change frequently.

All travellers
Polio and Tetanus/Diphtheria vaccinations should be up to date. All travellers need to ensure immunity to Measles, Mumps, Rubella and Chickenpox. Flu vaccine and Pneumonia vaccine are recommended for travellers over 65 years of age. HIB vaccine is recommended for travellers under 5 years.

Depending on where you go
Certain vaccines are recommended depending on which country you visit. For example:
* If you will be visiting a 'developing country' you will need Hepatitis A vaccine, even if only visiting resorts and 5 star hotels. You may also need typhoid vaccination especially if you plan to eat market or street stall food in these countries.
* Travellers to Nepal need Meningitis Vaccine.
Some vaccines are only necessary for visitors to certain parts of a country. For example:
* Yellow Fever Vaccine is needed for the Amazon Basin regions of Brazil, but not for Rio de Janeiro.

Depending on what you do while away
Certain vaccines are recommended depending on what you will do whilst away. For example:
* Travellers anticipating contact with blood products e.g. health care workers, should have Hepatitis B vaccine.
* Travellers who might have contact with animals, especially dogs, may need rabies vaccine.
* Travellers going to work in developing countries may need a TB test. Children may need the TB vaccine.
* Travellers going on cruises or bus tours may be recommended the influenza vaccine

Cholera is seldom required
The requirement for a cholera vaccination certificate was removed from the International Health Regulations in 1973. Some countries may still require a cholera stamp.

Special cases
Children, pregnant women, and those with medical conditions need to consult a travel doctor regarding which vaccinations are recommended.

How Long Vaccinations Last

The table below outlines the usual duration of protection once the vaccination course is complete. For some vaccines, the duration of protection is uncertain or a blood test is required after the course is completed.

Chickenpox (Varilrix)	?Life
Cholera (Orochol)	6 months
Diphtheria	10 years
Flu vaccine (Fluvax)	1 year
Hepatitis A (Vaqta/Havrix/Twinrix)	10-20 years
Hepatitis A (G Glob) 2mls	3 months
Hepatitis A (G Glob) 5mls	6 months
HepatitisB (HBVaxII/EngerixB/Twinrix)	?Life
Japanese B Encephalitis	3 years
Measles, Mumps, Rubella	?Life
Meningitis (Menomune/Mencevax)	1-3 years
Pneumonia (Pneumovax)	5 years
Polio (Sabin)	10 years
Rabies (pre exposure)	2-3 years
Tetanus	5 -10 years
Tuberculosis	Not known
Typhoid (Typhim Vi)	3 years
Typhoid capsules x 3	1 year
Typhoid capsules x 4	5 years
Typhoid (original injection)	3 years
Yellow Fever	10 years

How Vaccines are Given

POLIO
Sabin oral
Two drops of pink medicine. As long as the original course was given in childhood, the booster is only 2 drops on the tongue. (An injectible polio vaccine, IPOL is available for use in special circumstances.)

TETANUS
ADT / Tet Tox injection
Booster is one injection if the original course was given in childhood. Usually given combined with Diphtheria in ADT (Adult Diphtheria & Tetanus).

DIPHTHERIA
injection
Booster is one injection if the original course was given in childhood. Can be given separately but usually combined with Tetanus as ADT.

MEASLES
MUMPS
RUBELLA
MMR II injection
One injection protects against all three diseases.

CHICKENPOX
Varilrix injection
Two injections for adults who have not had the disease. One dose and then a second one in 6 weeks.

INFLUENZA
Fluvax injection
One injection only.

PNEUMONIA
Pneumovax injection
One injection only.

TYPHOID
Typhim Vi injection
One injection, preferably given at least 2 weeks before departure. This vaccine is now recommended instead of the original (old) typhoid vaccine because it generally has fewer side effects and requires one less injection.

Typh Vax Oral   Capsules
Three or four capsules, (depending on how long you wish to be protected from typhoid). Take one capsule every second day e.g. Day 1, 3, 5 (± 7). Take them on an empty stomach (2 hours after food), and don't eat for one hour after. Bedtime is the best time. *Tablets must be stored in the fridge.* No antibiotics or antimalarial tablets should be taken during this course, or for 1 week before or 1 week after this course.

HEPATITIS A   **Vaqta / Havrix injection**
One dose at 0, with a booster at 6-12 months.

Twinrix injection
Hepatitis A and B protection in the one vaccine.
One dose at 0, 1 month and 6 months.

Gamma Globulin injection
A blood product – seldom used any more.

MENINGITIS   **Menomune / Mencevax ACWY injection.**
One injection, given at least 2 weeks before travel.

YELLOW FEVER   **Stamaril injection**
One injection, given at least 10 days before travel.

CHOLERA   **Orochol oral**
Two sachets are emptied into 100mls of cold or
lukewarm water. Stir the mixture for 5-10 seconds and
drink immediately. Do not eat for one hour after.
Leave 8 hours between oral typhoid and orochol. Take
the mixture at least one week before travel.

JAPANESE B ENCEPHALITIS **JE Vax injection**
Three injections: Day 0, 7-14 and 28. The course must
be *completed* at least 10 days before leaving the
country.

HEPATITIS B   **HBVax II / Engerix B injection**
Usually three injections: at 0, 1 month and 6 months.
Rapid course may be 0, 1, 2, and 12 months. Usually
a blood test is recommended 4-6 weeks after the last
injection to confirm the vaccine has worked. If not,
further boosters are required. If required, Hepatitis A
and B protection, can be given in the same vaccine (see
Hepatitis A - Twinrix – above).

RABIES   **Human Diploid Cell Rabies injection**
Pre-bite protection (greatly simplifies treatment in the
event of a bite) three injections: one on day 0, 7, and
28. If bitten, a further two doses are required.

TUBERCULOSIS **BCG injection**
One injection. The vaccine does not work well in
adults. A Tuberculosis test (Mantoux) may be
recommended to document immunity before travel.
The test is then repeated after you return home.

Personal Vaccination Schedule
(To be filled in by your doctor)

eek?

DATE

Polio					
Tetanus/Diphtheria					
HIB					
Measles/Mumps/Rubella					
Chickenpox					
Flu					
Pneumonia					
Typhoid					
Hepatitis A					
Meningitis					
Yellow Fever					
Cholera					
Japanese B Encephalitis					
Hepatitis B					
Rabies					
Tuberculosis					
Malaria Tablets					

Don't forget your **travellers' medical kit** and a **letter of authorisation** for any pills, medications or drugs you will be carrying overseas.

Side Effects of Vaccination

What are the likely side effects?
These days, vaccines cause fewer problems than in the past. On the day of vaccination, most people can work, drive a car, play sport or go to the gym, but it is best to 'take it easy'. Modern vaccines do not leave a scar.

1. Fainting
The people most likely to faint are 20 to 29-year-old men of above average height, receiving a Tetanus or ADT vaccine plus another vaccine. If you have a history of fainting after injections, make sure you tell the doctor. You will need to lie down during vaccination and for up to ten minutes afterwards.

2. Allergic reactions (Anaphylaxis)
Allergic reactions are rare but may be very serious. After vaccinations, notify your doctor immediately if you feel...
* **warm**
* **itchy** (or develop a rash) away from the injection site
* **faint** (especially on standing up) or dizzy
* **short of breath**, or develop wheeze or cough
* swelling develop in throat, face, hands or limbs
* suddenly tired

Symptoms usually develop within 30 minutes of vaccination, (hence the need to wait in the clinic after receiving certain vaccines especially Yellow Fever). Occasionally allergic symptoms occur up to 10 days later (especially Japanese Encephalitis). If you develop one or more of the above symptoms within 10 days, immediately call your doctor or go to the nearest casualty department or well equipped medical centre.

Persons with allergies to eggs cannot have vaccines against Yellow Fever, Flu, and sometimes Measles/Mumps/Rubella. Travellers with penicillin allergy *can* be vaccinated safely.

3. Sore, red injection site
Usually vaccinations cause nothing more serious than a sore arm for a few days. If you keep your arm moving, it will help ease the soreness. The ADT injection may cause a deep lump or hardness which persists for a few weeks. If your arm is red, hot and/or sore, place an ice pack over the affected area. You may take paracetamol. Intradermal vaccines (e.g. Rabies) may cause itchiness at the injection site and a small surface lump which may persist for weeks.

4. Fevers and feeling sick

Yellow Fever vaccine (Stamaril) may cause a slight fever, headache, tiredness, and muscle aches in 2-10% of persons, starting 3-9 days after vaccination. MMR (Measles, Mumps, Rubella) may cause a fever in 5-15% of persons, starting 5-12 days after vaccination, along with a temporary rash in 5% persons. The old Typhoid/Cholera combination made many persons feel very 'unwell'. Most of the new 'dead' vaccines do not generally cause fevers. The Flu vaccine is 'dead' and cannot cause you to develop the Flu.

If you develop a fever or become unwell after vaccination, call the doctor who gave you the vaccines.

5. Diarrhoea or stomach problems

The oral Typhoid (capsules) may cause mild to moderate nausea, stomach cramps and diarrhoea within 12-24 hours after taking each capsule. If symptoms are more severe after the second capsule, call your doctor.

Will vaccines weaken my immune system?

Careful investigations have shown absolutely no evidence for any 'weakening'. The vaccines are a 'drop in the bucket' compared to what one's immune system is exposed to every day. A little bit of 'exercise' is probably very good for the immune system. Vaccinations are only recommended when the risk of the disease is far greater than that of the vaccine.

What if I have a cold?

It *is* safe to be vaccinated while you have a bit of a runny nose, sore throat or cough. Delay vaccination if you have a fever over 39°C or if you are sick enough to be in bed.

Can I drink alcohol after vaccines?

If you are having Japanese Encephalitis vaccine, you must avoid 'more than your usual' alcohol for 48 hours after each dose. If taking Typhoid capsules, alcohol (or food) must *not* be taken within a few hours of each capsule. However it *is* okay to have alcohol in the 48 hours after other vaccinations - however, stay under the legal limit - approximately one standard drink per hour.

The myth about "no alcohol after receiving vaccines" may have begun this way. Apparently army recruits used to be given numerous vaccines and then be given a day off to recover - and what did the army recruits do when they had the day off? They went to the pub and got drunk and obnoxious, so the army advised them not to drink any alcohol for 48 hours after their vaccines.

MALARIA PREVENTION

No tablet is 100% effective for preventing malaria.

1. Avoid mosquitoes.

2. Take malaria tablets regularly.

3. Treat fevers immediately.

1. Avoid Mosquitoes

On your trip
YOU may be
under attack!!

Don't let her bite you!
Malaria is transmitted by a female mosquito, which feeds at night - between dusk and dawn. *Day* biting mosquitoes transmit Dengue fever so *no* mosquito bite is safe. If possible, limit your exposure to all mosquitoes.

Cover up - long sleeved, light coloured clothes
If you are outside between dusk and dawn, wear treated long sleeved shirts, long pants, and long socks. Light coloured clothes are best - dark colours attract mosquitoes. Strong scents also attract mosquitoes, so avoid perfumes etc.

Use mosquito repellent regularly
'DEET' (Diethyl toluamide) is clinically proven to be the most effective mosquito repellent to apply on your skin e.g. Repel™ or Rid™. A concentration of 30% DEET is recommended for adults under conditions of intense mosquito exposure. Concentrations greater than 50% DEET are usually not recommended. Apply regularly as per instructions on the bottle.

When sunscreen is required, apply sunscreen first, wait 20 minutes and then apply repellent. Repellents decrease the number of bites you may get, but unfortunately, cannot stop mosquitoes entirely.

Sleeping precautions
Sleeping in air-conditioned or well - screened rooms is ideal. Use a 'knock down spray' to remove stray mosquitoes. Permethrin treated mosquito nets (see next page) are essential where the accommodation is not well screened. Check there are no holes in the net and tuck it in well. If there are mosquitoes already inside the net, spray them with insecticide before you go to bed. As a last resort burn mosquito coils, cover exposed skin in insect repellent, and sleep next to a fan.

Treating bed nets and clothes with Permethrin

What is Permethrin?

It is a highly effective synthetic insecticide, which can be used to treat fabric. Permethrin is related to the naturally occurring pyrethrum from the flowers of a type of Chrysanthemum. Treated fabric such as bed nets, bed sheets, clothes, or curtains kills or repels insects (e.g. mosquitoes).

Does it work?

Basically yes. Using treated items significantly decreases the number of bites you get. One study showed treated nets were **four** times more effective than untreated nets. Insects must touch the fabric for it to work, so when you wear treated clothes, you still need to use repellent on exposed skin. You can buy items pre-treated (especially bed nets) or treat items yourself with commercially produced Permethrin packs. Follow the treatment instructions carefully to get the full effect. Do not throw any excess down the sink as it is toxic to fish – throw it on the garden.

How long does it last?

Articles which are treated, and immediately sealed and stored in a plastic bag, will retain effectiveness for 12 months until usage is begun. A Permethrin impregnated mosquito net is effective for three to six months of regular use. The solution wears off as well as washes off. Clothes treated in this way are said to be fully active for about one month, remaining effective even after normal washing.

Is it safe?

Basically yes. Once the fabric is treated and dried, permethrin has no vapour action and nets can be safely used even around sleeping children. Should a young child suck the net, they will not suffer any ill effects. Treated items are not more flammable. Very occasionally, some people develop minor skin rashes from the use of treated clothes.

Oral vitamin B - does it help avoid mosquitoes?

Basically no. Taking large quantities of vitamin B orally *does not* decrease the number of mosquito bites you get. Such an apparently simple solution to mosquito avoidance is appealing, but careful scientific trials have failed to show any mosquito repelling effects from taking oral vitamin B, including B1.

There is some evidence that the use of B1 will make any bites feel less itchy, but the risk of picking up nasty diseases is just the same as if you did not take it.

2. Take Malaria tablets - which one?

There is no 'right' answer. The best choice for you depends on your past medical history, your destination(s), duration of stay, planned activities and your preference for possible side effects. Your doctor may recommend one of the following.

Chloroquine

Take 2 Chloroquine tablets *per week*, (e.g. every Monday). Start <u>2 weeks before</u> entering the malarial area, whilst there, and continue <u>until 4 weeks after</u> you leave the malarial risk area. Note: Do not take these tablets every day.

Mefloquine (Lariam)

Take one Mefloquine (Lariam) tablet *per week* (e.g. every Monday). Start <u>4 weeks before</u> entering the malarial area, take whilst there, and continue for <u>4 weeks after</u> leaving the malarial area. E.g. in weeks..

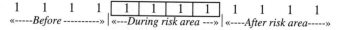

1   1   1   1 | 1 | 1 | 1 | 1 | 1   1   1   1

«-----*Before* ----------» | «---*During risk area* ---» | «----*After risk area*----»

If you experience side effects, try splitting the dose; take a half tablet twice a week (half on Monday, half on Thursday).

At the start of the course, your doctor may prescribe a 'loading dose' so you get useful blood levels more quickly. This is usually one tablet on day 0, 1, 2, 7, 14, 21 etc (one tablet on Monday, Tuesday, Wednesday, then every Monday).

Doxycycline

Take one **100mg** Doxycycline tablet *daily*. Start <u>2 days before</u> entering the area, take daily while there, and continue <u>for 14 days after</u>. It is important not to miss a single day.

Chloroquine and Paludrine

Take 2 tablets of Chloroquine *weekly* and 2 tablets of Paludrine *daily*. Start <u>2 weeks before</u> entering the malarial area, take while in the risk area, and continue for <u>4 weeks after</u> you leave the malaria risk area.

Malarone

Take 1 tablet *daily*. Start <u>2 days before</u> entering the malarial area, take while in the risk area and continue <u>until 7 days after</u> leaving the risk area.

No regular prevention pills

Take no regular pills, but avoid mosquitoes, and treat fevers urgently if they develop. It may be necessary to carry emergency malaria standby treatment (see pp 79-83).

How to take Malaria tablets

With Food !!!!
You will have fewer side effects if you take your tablets with a large glass of water and a meal; have some of your meal, take your tablets and then finish your meal.

Same day each week
Weekly tablets must be taken on the same day each week. e.g. "Monday is Malaria day". Use the same day as your fellow travellers to help you remember.

To the bitter end
If you stop your tablets early you may get Malaria. These tablets are not like regular antibiotics - they take many weeks to kill malarial parasites.

If you forget a dose
1. Weekly tablets. Take the missed tablet the day you remember. If you are only one day late, subsequent tablets can be taken on your 'usual' day. If more than one day late, you need to take subsequent doses one week later - on the new day.
2. Daily tablets. Take the tablet the day you remember and continue daily doses. Do not take extra tablets per day to make up for the ones you missed.
If you have missed tablets you may get malaria. If fever develops, remember you must see a doctor ASAP.

Alcohol
You may drink alcohol in moderation while taking malaria tablets. However, heavy alcohol consumption within 24 hours of a dose of Lariam (mefloquine) is likely to provoke hallucinations, behaviour changes or even epileptic fits.

Do they have side effects?
Unfortunately yes. Research by TMVC has found that up to 40% of people taking malaria pills will get side effects. Usually these side effects are minor, and do not mean that you should stop your pills.

Test your tablets before departure, so if they cause problems you can discuss it with the doctor *before* you go. Sometimes the type of tablet, or dosage may need to be changed. The following section describes potential side effects of various tablets. Some travellers believe hair loss is a side effect of malaria pills, however this is more likely to be caused by prolonged, stressful travelling. If in doubt, speak to your doctor.

Side effects of Malaria tablets

Unfortunately there is no malaria tablet which is perfectly effective and perfectly safe. If the risk of malaria is very low, you are more likely to get sick from your tablets than get malaria, so it is *not worth taking tablets*. However if the malaria risk is high, putting up with minor side effects is *preferable* to catching cerebral malaria and dying.

Chloroquine

Chloroquine tastes bitter. Some people notice mild nausea and headache the day they take the tablets. Dehydration will make the symptoms worse so drink extra water. A dose of paracetamol will also help. Splitting the dose (rather than two on Monday, take one tablet Monday and one on Thursday) will often alleviate side effects. Temporary blurry vision may be noted after the first one or two doses. Provided you have regular checkups, chloroquine is safe to take continually for several years and does not cause eye damage. Chloroquine is even safe in pregnancy. Although safe at recommended doses, chloroquine is extremely toxic if an overdose is taken - a few tablets will kill a small child.

Chloroquine comes in 2 forms: Chloroquine *Phosphate* 250 mg and Chloroquine *Sulphate* 200mg. Both preparations contain 150 mg of 'base', i.e. the same amount of actual Chloroquine. Chloroquine sulphate should be avoided in some people with sulphur allergies.

Mefloquine (Lariam)

Although Mefloquine (Lariam) is very effective, it causes troublesome side effects in up to 15% of users. The effects usually occur with the first few doses, so you need to start these tablets four weeks before travel. Mefloquine users often describe trouble sleeping and strange dreams - one lady kept dreaming her tent was filling with quicksand. It has also been reported to cause dizziness, feelings of disorientation, confusion, mood swings, anxiety, depression, nausea, stomach discomfort, visual disturbance and palpitations. These effects are most unpleasant but are reversible on stopping the drug. *Do not take Mefloquine on an empty stomach or within 24 hours of heavy alcohol use* or these symptoms will be much worse. Side effects (if any) will develop more quickly if you take the loading dose.

Travellers with a history of psychiatric or seizure disorders must never take Mefloquine. Approximately one in 10,000 users will have an epileptic fit. If unexplained anxiety, depression, hallucinations or confusion occurs, you must stop taking this drug immediately and see a doctor.

Mefloquine may interfere with tasks requiring fine coordination. It should not be taken by pilots or scuba divers. Driving cars is considered safe, but as a precaution, avoid driving for 24 hours after the first four test doses, until you are sure you feel okay.

Mefloquine theoretically interacts with some blood pressure or migraine tablets (especially the group known as Beta Blockers). Quinine (e.g. used for cramps) should not be taken at the same time as Mefloquine. If in doubt, ask the doctor. Mefloquine is usually not recommended for small children (<15 kg) or in the first third of pregnancy. Women should use reliable contraception while taking it, and for three months after the last dose. Mefloquine *is* sometimes recommended in the last two thirds of pregnancy if the woman and foetus will be at extreme risk of Malaria.

This medication has received a great deal of bad publicity. It is certainly not a perfect drug, and is most useful in areas where the malaria risk is extreme.

Doxycycline

It is most important to take doxycycline *with food* or it will cause irritation of the oesophagus, felt as pain or burning in the centre of the chest. Do not take doxycycline immediately before going to bed or even lying down. It is preferable to avoid antacids (e.g. Mylanta) whilst taking doxycycline.

Some people on this drug develop a red rash in areas exposed to light. This rash may tingle or burn. It is especially common on the back of the hands. This rash or photosensitivity is not really sunburn, but it pays to avoid excessive sun while taking this medication. Nail abnormalities have also been described.

If you are allergic to Tetracycline drugs you cannot take doxycycline. This drug is a broad-spectrum antibiotic. Women prone to vaginal itching or thrush after antibiotics, should carry a supply of anti-thrush medication (e.g. econazole) just in case. There is also a very small chance it may interfere with the contraceptive effect of 'the pill'. Children who are under 8 years of age, and pregnant women should not take doxycycline as it stains growing teeth. Pregnancy should be avoided for seven days after ceasing this drug.

Paludrine

Paludrine is one of the safest malaria tablets available. It is even safe in pregnancy. Mouth ulcers are more common while taking Paludrine.

3. Treat fevers immediately

You need an urgent blood test if you develop a fever during or after visiting a malaria risk area.

You can still catch Malaria despite taking Malaria pills.

The most important symptom to watch for is fever, or 'having a temperature'. Normal body temperature is 37°C.

Any fever should be treated as malaria, until proven otherwise. Malaria can be diagnosed by a simple blood test carried out on a finger prick of blood.

Malaria can be completely cured if treated early.

Malaria can be fatal if left untreated for only 3 days.

If you develop **a temperature greater than 38°C** during or after visiting a malaria risk area, you must **see a doctor as soon as possible**... whether you are taking malaria tablets or not!

TRAVELLERS MEDICAL KIT

Many people are tempted to think -
"I won't need all this stuff" but the fact is that 50% of travellers experience medical concerns on their trip.

Be prepared just in case. Your kit doesn't have to be huge to be very useful. It is especially important to be prepared if you are travelling independently, without the safety net of a package tour and guide. What you will need depends on where you are going, what you will be doing, and your past medical history. You can make up your own kit or buy a ready made one. The following list will help you plan your medical kit. Discuss medical supplies with your doctor. You will not need everything listed but *indicates the most commonly used items.

All travellers
*Your regular medications, even if you only use them occasionally at home. Take spare supplies.
*Digital thermometer (mercury thermometers are difficult to read, and mercury is not allowed on some aeroplanes).
*Vaccination certificate, especially if you have been vaccinated against Yellow Fever
*Travel insurance with good medical cover for emergencies
*Important documents and photocopies/details of these, especially passport, air tickets, vaccination certificate, creditcards, phone card.
Money clip to use as decoy (see p62)

If sexually active
Condoms
Water soluble lubricant e.g. KY

To avoid mosquito carried diseases
*Mosquito repellent for personal use
Long sleeved, light coloured clothes for evenings
Permethrin treated clothes (shirts, socks) may be useful
Bed nets treated with permethrin
Mosquito coils
'Knock down' insect spray to kill mosquitoes inside tents etc
Malaria tablets if prescribed
Malaria test kit if travelling to remote areas

To prevent sun damage
*Blockout/sunscreen (15+ at least) for lips and body
*Sunglasses and hat

To ensure safe water
Water purification - Iodine tablets, alum, vitamin C powder
Water purifier e.g. PentaPure™ or PUR™ products
Clean and sturdy one litre water bottle
Clean straws

To treat stomach problems
* Rehydration sachets (Gastrolyte blackcurrant flavour is best)
* Loperamide (Imodium) - temporary 'stopper' for diarrhoea
* Norfloxacin (Noroxin) - antibiotic kills most diarrhoea germs
* Tinidazole (Fasigyn) - antibiotic kills giardia diarrhoea germs
* Maxolon or Stemetil – to treat nausea
* Antispasmodic e.g. Buscopan
BactrimDS - antibiotic for cyclospora diarrhoea germs
Indigestion tablets e.g. Quick-eze, Mylanta
Laxative e.g. Coloxyl + fibre supplement e.g. Metamucil

To treat wounds/skin infections
*Dressings - bandaids, elastoplast, Opsite, non stick dressing,
gauze, crepe bandage, sling, SoloSite gel, Steristrips, tape
*Antiseptic e.g. Betadine cream
Antibiotics for wound infections e.g. cephalexin
Anti-fungal Cream/Powder e.g. clotrimazole
Blister prevention/treatment e.g. Compeed, Moleskin
Cold sore cream e.g. Stoxil, Zovirax

To treat aches and pains
*Painkillers e.g. paracetamol, codeine, aspirin
Anti-inflammatory tablets e.g. piroxicam, ibuprofen

To treat coughs, colds, sinus, chest infections
*Nasal decongestant e.g. pseudoephedrine tablets, nasal spray
*Throat lozenges e.g. Difflam, Cepacol, Strepsils
Cough capsules e.g. Orthoxicol
*Antibiotic e.g. roxithromycin (Rulide), amoxycillin

To treat allergies / insect bites
Anti-histamine tablets e.g. promethazine (Avomine), Zyrtec
Stingose gel
Steroid cream e.g. Diprosone, Betnovate

To treat eye problems
Antibiotic cream or drops to treat conjunctivitis, especially
for contact lens wearers e.g. Chloromycetin, Soframycin
An empty film canister to use as an eye bath
Eye drops (Polytears free, Visine) for wind/glare/dust
A spare pair of glasses or a copy of your prescription

To treat ear problems
Aqua-ear to dry ear canal
Antibiotic drops/cream e.g. Sofradex

To assist plane travel / avoid jet lag
Mild sleeping tablets e.g. temazepam (Normison)
Eye mask/neck pillow
Lollies / candy to relieve ear pain from cabin pressure changes
Earplugs (Earplanes) - relieve ear pain from pressure changes
Compression stockings to stop blood clots in the leg if at risk

Medical Equipment
Sterile needles and syringes in different sizes
Scissors, tweezers, splinter probe
Dental emergency kit / oil of cloves/ temporary filling

Other useful things to consider
Vitamins - especially vitamins B and C
Moisturiser e.g. Vaseline
Lip balm e.g. Bepanthen
Dental floss and sealed container for your toothbrush
Antiseptic hand wash e.g. Microshield
Swiss army knife, cup and spoon, small torch
Sturdy needle and thread, safety pins of various sizes
Scarf/mask- to cover nose & mouth if visiting dusty places
Packaged food e.g. dried fruit, biscuits, snack bars
Toilet paper - in short supply in some developing countries
Thongs/footwear - to wear in communal showers, hostels etc
Disposable ear plugs for sleeping in noisy tea houses/hotels
NapiSan to clean and sterilise when washing clothes
Insecticide treated sleep sheet to avoid bedbugs
Waders, waterproof boots/gloves (to avoid schistosomiasis)

If going to high altitude places
Acetazolamide (Diamox)

If going on cruises or boats
Motion sickness medication e.g. hyoscine (SCOP, Kwells)
promethazine, drammamine, ginger
Non-slip shoes and extra sunscreen

If going on surfing trips
Plenty of antiseptic, non-stick dressings, moist dressings
New soft toothbrush to clean coral cuts, hydrogen peroxide
Antibiotics for infected coral cuts e.g. cephalexin (Keflex)
Vinegar for marine stings

If going on important business trips
Consider antibiotics to prevent traveller's diarrhoea

Women travellers

Adequate supplies of tampons/sanitary pads - (they are hard to obtain or expensive in some parts of world)
Medication for period pains - Ponstan, Naprogesic
Adequate supplies of the contraceptive pill
Emergency contraception (morning-after pill)
Treatment for vaginal thrush - econazole pessaries, fluconazole
Treatment for cystitis/bladder infection e.g. citravescent, ural, or an antibiotic e.g. trimethoprim, norfloxacin

Pregnant travellers

Paracetamol
Rehydration solution (e.g. Gastrolyte)
Anti-embolism stockings (e.g. T.E.D. ^{TM}) for long journeys
Antibiotic for respiratory or bladder infection
Vitamins (in the first 12 weeks you should take folic acid)
Snack food

Children travellers

Rehydration solution (e.g. Gastrolyte)
Infant or child paracetamol
Medicine for colds or runny noses e.g. Dimetapp
Antihistamine for insect bites and sedation on planes - make sure you test it on the child before the day of departure
Calamine lotion/Stingose gel
Aqua Ear to prevent 'tropical ear' after swimming
Adequate supplies of dressings and antiseptic
Some favourite foods or snacks
Some new and entertaining toys, and a familiar toy
Vitamin drops if food will be poor quality/fluoride tablets
Large container to sterilise bottles etc plus sterilising tablets
Nappy rash cream/teething gel if relevant
Plenty of baby wipes, antiseptic hand wash etc.
A change of clothes for the carer in case the child vomits (or worse!) on you while travelling
(NB Antibiotics are not on this list as it is not recommended to give a child antibiotics without medical supervision)

Ready made kits

If you don't want to fiddle about making up your own kit, a range of ready made Travellers Medical Kits - suitable for every type of trip and traveller - are available from the Travel Doctor group These must be prescribed by a doctor and contain both dressings and 'drugs'. They are more economical than buying individual items separately.

Check out http://www.traveldoctor.com.au

Useful facts about travelling with drugs

Keep drugs away from children
Always keep drugs out of the reach of children. Even a few malaria tablets can kill a baby.

Instructions
Carry written instructions for all medications, so you know what they are for and how to take them.

Letter of Authorisation
Any medications carried overseas should be accompanied by a covering letter from a doctor. This is especially important if you carry needles and syringes for emergency use.

Several years ago a young woman was jailed in Greece for carrying headache tablets containing codeine.

Misunderstandings may be avoided by carrying the correct paperwork. Travellers sometimes wonder if a letter is *really* necessary for simple things like paracetamol. Many travellers carry these letters and very few are actually asked to produce them. You will not be routinely asked to show your letter of authorisation, but if a customs official is going through your bag and discovers a pile of little pink pills, it is best to have authorisation. If you are going through customs you may be asked (e.g. in the paperwork) whether you are carrying any 'drugs or medications'. You could answer 'Yes, On doctor's advice' - but only if it is true!)

Storage
Drug expiry dates are not reliable if medicines have been incorrectly stored. Place medications together in a suitable container. Ideally the container should be labelled – 'first aid kit' or 'travellers medical kit'. A white cross on a green background is the recognised symbol for a first aid kit. A label like this will make your kit look more 'official'.

While travelling, try to protect your kit from extremes of temperature. Medications must be kept cool and dry - they will deteriorate unpredictably in hot or damp conditions. Don't leave the kit sitting in the hot sun for hours on end (e.g. in your backpack). It is best to carry essential medications in your hand luggage; illness can strike at any time. Your kit must be waterproof (soggy tablets will not work).

Obtaining medications overseas

Home prescriptions *cannot* be filled overseas. Take what you may need from home. It is better to avoid 'the little red pills' given to you by fellow travellers, maids, bus drivers or other unqualified people.

If possible, avoid purchasing medications in foreign countries. In many areas of the world, drugs have been altered or mislabelled, and often they are out of date. If you must obtain drugs overseas, buy them from large stores in major cities. Many developing countries sell restricted drugs without prescription. Make sure you know what you are buying. Some medications contain things which may be dangerous if taken inappropriately. Avoid the following potentially dangerous tablets: Chloramphenicol, Butazolidin, Aminopyrine, Enterovioform, Clioquinol. Drug names are often different in other countries. You may wish to refer to the reference table at the back of this book.

Sharing drugs

Try to avoid sharing medications with fellow travellers, they may have allergies of which you are unaware, but most importantly you may need those drugs later yourself.

Know your blood group

For long-term travellers it may be handy to know your blood group, and that of your fellow travellers.

The likelihood of needing a blood transfusion during international travel is very low. It has been estimated at 13 per 100,000 travellers per fortnight.

Medical Insurance

It is strongly recommended all travellers take out travel insurance to cover medical evacuation and illness overseas.

A 24 hour phone number for emergencies is very useful. If you have existing medical conditions e.g. asthma, if you are pregnant, or if you are planning any activities like skiing, scuba diving, motor bike riding, hang gliding etc. read the policy carefully to see whether you are covered before buying the insurance.

Those going to live and work in developing countries need a special type of long term health insurance, which covers more than just the emergency medical care.

PRE - TRAVEL CHECKUPS
1. Dental

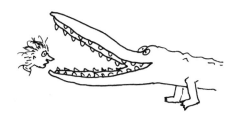

Visit the Dentist
If you have not had a check up in the last six months, go now.
You should mention to your dentist where you are going and
for how long.

Three months before departure
Aim to visit well before departure, so there is time for
necessary dental work to be done. Your dentist may suggest
X-rays if you will be away for more than six months. This
will detect problems in the early stages. A loose filling may
cause considerable pain if you fly in an unpressurised aircraft
or scuba dive. You should avoid air travel for three days after
extensive dental work.

A dental checkup before departure is essential if you are
visiting countries where dental services are poor.

Dentures
Carry a spare set in case dentures get damaged or lost.

Fluoride
Children on fluoride supplements should not stop them when
they are overseas.

Container for your toothbrush
While you are away, avoid placing your toothbrush on
bathroom counters, or unclean surfaces. Germs can be picked
up in this way, and quickly transferred to your mouth.

2. Medical Checkup

All travellers

If you will be away for longer than six months, or travelling to places with poor medical services you should ensure there are no potential medical problems brewing. For example; if you have any symptoms you have been meaning to get checked, or any skin lesions which have changed – have them examined wellbefore departure. Women should ensure smear tests etc. are up to date. Some travellers may need blood tests.

If you have a pre-existing medical condition

Check with your doctor before you travel if you have diabetes, asthma, heart disease, epilepsy, mental illness, HIV or any other chronic disease.

For example; persons with a history of asthma need a written asthma management plan from their doctor. This will outline which medication to take, and in what order if their asthma symptoms worsen. The plan may include the use of oral steroids if travellers will be visiting very isolated areas.

Migraine sufferers should take plenty of their usual pain killers, sleeping tablets, anti-nausea pills etc. Discuss with your doctor whether you would be suitable for sumatriptan (Imigran) or one of the derivatives. They are expensive but act quickly to stop the migraine, rather than just killing the pain.

Carry written details of important medical history

Carry a letter from your doctor giving details of any medical condition you have, and the usual treatment such as the drug and dosage. Drug allergies and blood group (if known) should be noted. Take adequate supplies of your usual medications.

Physically demanding trips

If you will be exerting yourself more than usual, it is wise to have a medical clearance before departure. Trekkers over 40 years of age may need an exercise cardiograph (ECG). This is a test of your heart's performance during exercise, and may uncover potential problems before you leave.

Scubadivers

If you are going scuba diving for the first time, ensure you have a medical from a doctor certified or experienced in diving medicine before you leave home.

Pregnant travellers

If you are healthy, well organised and determined then your pregnancy will not be a barrier to travel. If this is your first baby it may be your last chance to travel unfettered!

Where to go while pregnant?

It is best to discuss your destination with your doctor *before* travel plans are finalised. Pregnant travellers can safely visit many places, but *travel to malarious areas is not safe during pregnancy.* Malaria is more serious in pregnant women. Malaria can cause miscarriage. The most effective malaria tablets are not safe during pregnancy.

Most pregnancies progress absolutely normally, but travel to developing countries where medical services are unreliable may spell disaster if complications develop. It is safer to visit countries where medical care is of high standard.

What stage of pregnancy is best for travel?

The middle third of pregnancy is the safest time to travel. After the first 12-16 weeks, the risk of miscarriage is low, and morning sickness is usually over. After 28 weeks you will have a big tummy, and be more uncomfortable. You will probably start to need an afternoon nap and your feet may swell quite considerably during air travel. Airlines generally refuse to carry women over 36 weeks pregnant. In the last third of pregnancy it is wise to be close to good medical care in case it is needed.

Vaccination during pregnancy

Some vaccines can be safely given to pregnant women. Live vaccines are best avoided during pregnancy as they may cause disease in the developing child. You need to discuss your itinerary and vaccinations with your doctor.

Particular challenges for pregnant travellers

If this is your first pregnancy, read up about what to expect as the weeks progress. Pregnancy makes you hungry, more easily tired, and your bladder needs constant emptying. Plan ahead. Organise your journey so you have plenty of time for rest. Carry snacks in case you can't find decent food. Dress conveniently for frequent trips to the toilet. Try to eat a balanced diet. Depending on where you are going, you may need vitamin supplements. Ask the doctor which ones are suitable.

During pregnancy, the immune system may be somewhat overloaded (trying to safeguard two instead of one) so you are more prone to illness. Be particularly careful choosing food and drink. It is miserable to be pregnant and sick, and many medications are not recommended during pregnancy. Fever also increases the risk of miscarriage.

Newborn babies

It is best to wait until a baby is at least 6 weeks old before taking them on a plane and exposing them to the gamut of infectious organisms in air conditioning systems etc. Vaccines can be started early if necessary. TB and Hepatitis B vaccine can be given at birth.

If possible, breastfeeding is particularly helpful when travelling. It provides a convenient supply of clean and nutritious food, along with a constant supply of antibodies from the mother to help protect the child from illness. If planning to take medications while breastfeeding, remember to check that they will not get through the milk and harm the baby.

Travelling with children

Proximity to good medical care is important when travelling with children. The immune system of a child is more fragile than that of an adult. It may be preferable to wait until a child is two years old before taking non-essential trips to isolated parts of the developing world, but each case has to be taken on its merits.

Ensure all childhood vaccines are up to date.

Taking unvaccinated children overseas exposes them to serious risk. In Australia they are protected from disease by 'herd' immunity - everyone around them is immune so they are not exposed to the germs. It is interesting to note that the Council of the Faculty of Homoeopathy in London strongly supports the standard immunisation program for children and has stated that vaccination carried out in the normal way is consistent with homoeopathic principles.

Plan your trip so the schedule is not too hectic and there is time for the children to play. This will make everyone happier.

FITNESS TRAINING

Who?

 YOU!!

Yes! Everyone will benefit! The fitter you are, the more you will enjoy your trip. It is especially important if you are planning strenuous activities on your journey such as trekking, bicycling, rafting, diving, skiing. The benefits will far outweigh the pre-travel effort.

Why?

You will decrease your risk of injuries and other health problems if you are physically fit.

When?

You should start at least 8 weeks before departure.

What?

General exercise: walking, bushwalking, cycling, gym classes, swimming, or other sports.

Specific training: the best training is practising what you will be doing when away e.g. walking for a walking trip, cycling for a cycling trip, swimming for a dive trip.

Trekking: if you are going trekking, you really need to practise walking up hills, preferably with a pack. Walking up and down hills will give you specific fitness and accustom your joints to the "up and down travel". It will also wear in your shoes!

First aid course

Knowledge of basic first aid may help you save a friend's life. Undertaking a first aid course is a wise investment in your health abroad, especially when planning trips to isolated areas in developing countries. Courses are run by organisations such as the Australian Red Cross, St John's Ambulance Australia, Royal Life Saving Society, and Surf Life Saving Australia. See your local phone book for contact details.

JET LAG PREVENTION

You need not get off the plane feeling like a Zombie.

Stopovers
Discuss with your travel agent the possibility of a stopover in your journey, especially if travelling EAST.
Jet lag is said to be worse when travelling Eastward.

Night arrival
If possible, plan to arrive late so it will be time to sleep.

Plan to do nothing for the first 24hrs
Don't organise much to do on the first day after you arrive.

Will you need a special meal?
Non standard meals e.g. vegetarian, low fat, or children's meals, can be ordered for the journey.

A special seat?
If you have medical problems which worsen on prolonged sitting, or if you are pregnant you should request an aisle seat. This allows easier mobility for stretching the legs. Non smoking seats can be requested in advance, although many airlines are now non smoking (ask your travel agent).

Start your journey well rested if possible
Two good night's sleep before you go is ideal. Have your big farewell party some days before leaving if possible.

Melatonin – a magic cure?
Melatonin is a brain hormone which controls the body's internal clock (levels go up when it is dark and it makes you sleepy). A great deal of research is being undertaken on this compound to clarify its use in jetlag. In the United States melatonin outsells vitamin C - it is promoted for many things including to 'stop aging'. At present Melatonin cannot be recommended for all travellers to minimise jetlag; some persons feel better, some feel no different and some feel worse! No dose recommendations have been finalised, manufacturing is poorly standardised and currently the drug is not readily available in Australia, except via the Internet.

PACKING

Travel light

Be absolutely ruthless. First time travellers always take too much stuff (it is most unlikely you will need more than 3 pairs of shoes). Ask a well-travelled friend to check your luggage before the final pack. They will be more aware of what you will really need. Excess luggage is a definite health hazard. It can cause strained backs and nerves.

Luggage

You *will* have to carry your luggage at some stage. There is never a trolley, or porter, around when you need them. Use a suitcase with wheels, or a pack, depending on your style of trip. Suitcase wheels should be sturdy. The suitcase strap or handle should be long enough so you do not hunch over when pulling it. The pack should be comfortable and well fitted.

Clothing for the journey

Wear comfortable clothes, and roomy, comfortable shoes. Your feet may swell during flight.

Hand luggage for the plane

Make sure your hand luggage fits under the seat, or in the overhead locker, and does not cramp your available leg space. Consider the following for your hand luggage:

Valuables
Money belt, tickets, travellers cheques, passport, vaccination book, phone card, credit cards, foreign cash.
Medical kit
Medical kit including your usual prescription medicines. Luggage does go astray.
Glasses
Eye glasses, contact lenses, carry case and solution, spare lens prescription.
Toiletries
Moisturiser for face and lips, toothbrush and paste, deodorant, brush or comb etc.
Other
A jumper (and change of clothes if travelling with small children).
Compression stockings for those at risk of clots in the leg.
An eye mask and travel pillow will help you to sleep.
Things to do - especially if travelling with young children - e.g. pen, paper, reading material, games, knitting, computer
A bottle of water

WHILE YOU ARE AWAY

DURING THE FLIGHT

Exercise
Get up and walk around every hour or so. This stops blood pooling in your legs and lowers your risk of the very serious medical problem called DVT (Deep Vein Thrombosis) or clots in the leg. These are more common in tall persons over 50 years of age after 12 hours of flying. Do the stretches and exercises on the following page. Exercise also helps prevent swollen feet. This is especially important if you are pregnant - your feet may swell even if they have never swelled before.

Drink liquids
The air in a plane is very drying. One glass of liquid every hour will help maintain your body fluids. Fruit juice and water are best. Avoid fizzy drinks. As cabin air pressure goes down, any gas in your stomach will expand by as much as 20%. This will make you feel bloated.

Alcohol in moderation
Excess alcohol will make dehydration worse (also it tends to immobilise one and increase the risk of thrombosis).

Eat sparingly
Your body needs LESS food than normal when you are just sitting.

No smoking
There is less oxygen available in the air on a plane. Smoking will lower your oxygen still further, making you feel even more tired and wrung out. Many airlines no longer allow smoking during the flight.

Sitting position
Remove bulky objects from your back pocket. Put a pillow in the small of your back. Crossing your legs interferes with the circulation and puts uneven strain on different parts of the body so minimise this if you can.

Sleeping
Use your eye mask to block out the light. A travel pillow will reduce neck strain from sleeping upright. Listening to familiar music may also help you sleep. If you take a sleeping tablet then take it close to night time in the country of your destination. This will help you adjust more quickly to the new time zones. Avoid sleeping during descent. Sleep decreases the number of times you swallow. Swallowing helps equalise the pressure changes in your ears as the plane descends.

In Flight Exercises
Ideally these should be performed every few hours.

Feet circling
Circle your feet at the ankles - 20 times each foot.

Bottom lifts
Lift one buttock off the seat, feeling the muscles on that side tighten. Hold to the count of 5. Do 5 each side.

Knee presses
Press knees and thighs together and tighten buttock muscles. Hold to the count of 5. Do 5 each side.

Back presses
Press small of your back into the seat, letting your shoulders come forward. Alternate with pressing your shoulders into the seat. Do this 5 times.

Shoulder circles
With arms at sides, circle shoulders forwards 10 times, then backwards 10 times.

Head circles
Slowly circle your head in one direction, then the other. Repeat 10 times.

Head presses
Link fingers together, place arms behind your head with your elbows pointing forward. Gently push your head into your hands. Hold for count of five. Do this 5 times.

Heel/toe presses
Lift heels and press toes into the floor, then lift your toes and press your heels into the floor. 10 times each foot.

IF PEOPLE LOOK AT YOU STRANGELY...... Smile and encourage them to do the exercises as well.

ADAPTING TO NEW TIME ZONES

Rest
Take it easy. Try to avoid a lot of driving, making big decisions or doing strenuous tours the first day. You will not be at your peak. The best cure for jet lag is rest.

Three clues
When you arrive at the new time zone, you will adapt faster if you try to do what the locals are doing. Your body uses the following clues to set its internal clock:

1. Sunshine
A walk in the sunshine on the morning after arrival stimulates the optic nerve and helps the pineal gland in your head reset the body clock.

2. Meal times
Your body uses food as a clue to the time of day. Eat something at the new meal times to get your body on the right track. Avoid caffeine drinks after 4.00pm. The caffeine can keep you awake for many hours afterwards.

3. Sleeping times
Try to sleep at the new times. If you are very tired in the middle of the day have a *short* nap. Set an alarm. If you cannot sleep the first night, try taking some calcium or a high carbohydrate snack before bedtime e.g. five marshmallows. This increases brain serotonin which helps cause drowsiness. A mild sleeping pill e.g. temazepam may be useful.

Flying Australia to London
Most flights to the UK arrive first thing in the morning. You may arrive in London after 26 hours or more in the air. The clocks say 6.00am. whereas in Australia it's about 2.00pm. It is difficult to stay awake another sixteen hours until *local* bedtime if you have not slept on the plane. If you can have a decent sleep on the plane before arrival, you will feel more like it really *is* 6.00am. You may need to take a sleeping tablet e.g. temazepam seven hours before landing to help you sleep on the plane.

After arrival go for a walk in the sunshine (if there is any). Eat your meals at the English times. Your body will adjust to the new time zones more quickly if you do as the locals do; especially eating and sleeping at the appropriate times.

Time Zone Map

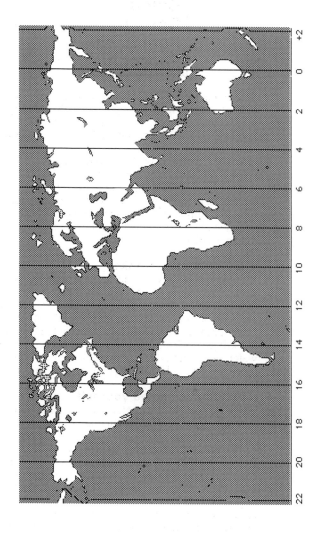

'GASTRO' PREVENTION

Safe Eating

> **Boil it,
> Cook it,
> Peel it, or
> Forget it!**

Safe eating means you cannot always eat *when* you want. It is better to miss a meal through choice than through illness! It may sound obvious, but germs are invisible and tasteless. Food which is absolutely infested can look and taste delicious.

Recently cooked, well cooked food
Germs are killed by thorough cooking. Meat, rice or vegetables which are hot all the way through, are safest. If your food is eaten immediately after cooking, germs have no time to multiply. Food which has been cooked in advance, and then left to sit at room temperature is a common cause of food poisoning.

Bottled or canned drinks
If buying water, always check the seal on the bottle, and buy from a reputable source. Enterprising locals may refill old bottles with local water and sell them as 'treated'. Beer, wine, and carbonated drinks are safe. Milk should be canned. Never drink unpasteurised milk. Alcohol in a mixed drink will not kill germs from the water or ice. When you buy bottled water, don't drink directly from the bottle if your mouth will touch the dirty sides; carry straws or a clean cup.

Fruit you have peeled yourself
Thick skinned fruit is preferable, so you do not contaminate the fruit as you peel it. Bananas are a great standby.

Clean hands and clean utensils
Before handling any food, you need to wash your hands with soap and water. Tap water is safe to wash hands. If this is not available, you can use antiseptic hand wash (e.g. Microshield™) or pour a little Dettol™ onto some wet wipes and use that to clean your hands. Check that plates and cutlery are clean. Don't eat off wooden chopsticks as they cannot be washed properly.

Unsafe Eating

DANGER!

Local water
Don't ever drink from streams. Avoid tap water in developing countries, especially in the rural areas. Don't clean your teeth or open your mouth in the shower either! The tap water in Western Europe, USA, UK, Australia and New Zealand and other similar countries is safe.

Ice
Avoid ice unless it is made with treated water. Ice in drinks or cocktails is a common cause of travellers diarrhoea. Freezing preserves germs, rather than killing them.

Raw or undercooked food
Raw food should be avoided. Cooking kills germs. Raw vegetables in a 'healthy' looking salad may actually be very unhealthy. Human manure is used to fertilise growing vegetables in some areas. Salad items may be infectious if washed in local water. Avoid cold, raw or undercooked meat of any kind. It may be contaminated with bacteria or parasites. You might pick up tape worms which can live in your gut for ten years. It is best to politely decline dishes containing raw or undercooked eggs e.g. home made mayonnaise, hollandaise sauce and desserts such as mousse.

Room temperature or reheated food
Be suspicious of food which has been left at room temperature for some time, or food which has been cooked and reheated.

Shellfish and seafood
Avoid raw seafood. Seafood may have grown in sewage polluted waters. Raw oysters and cold, previously cooked prawns are especially risky. Well cooked, recently prepared seafood is usually safe. Avoid eating large tropical reef fish as these can cause ciguatera poisoning.

Dairy products
If refrigeration is not reliable, dairy products are dangerous. Tinned milk is okay. Avoid unpasteurised milk, custards, ice creams, and creamy desserts. Milk and dairy products are usually safe if served by a five star hotel.

Safe Drinking Water

Clean water is fundamental to good health while travelling. It is essential to use safe water for drinking, cleaning your teeth, washing wounds, and washing food. Bottled water is usually readily available and convenient. It is safe, provided it is bottled by a reputable source, as previously noted. Unfortunately the disposal of used plastic water bottles is a major environmental problem.

To disinfect your own water you can use the following methods.

Boiling

Boiling water for *one minute* will ensure water is safe to drink, even at altitude. For every 300m of altitude, water boils at 1°C less. For example, at 3000m (10,000ft) water boils at 90°C. This is still adequate to kill cysts, bacteria, parasites and viruses, and prevent gastroenteritis. The time bringing the water to the boil, and cooling afterwards is an important part of the purifying process. Heat is a simple, time-honoured, one step method for ensuring safe water.

Chemical Disinfection - Iodine

Iodine (Potable Aqua™) is a more reliable chemical for water purification than chlorine or silver. Chlorine (Puritabs™) may fail if water is heavily contaminated. Silver (Micropur™) is not active against worm eggs, amoebae or viruses.

Iodine has been used continuously for up to 3 years in adults with no ill effects, but some authorities recommend a maximum of 6 months of continuous use. Iodine is not recommended for persons with known iodine allergy, unstable thyroid disease, or for more than 3 weeks in pregnant women.

Unfortunately, complete *chemical* purification of dirty water is a two step process (three if you want the water to taste good). Iodine tablets alone may be acceptable only for high quality source water e.g. from hotel taps.

Step 1. Cloudy or dirty water must be cleared first. Clarification removes unpleasant colour, taste, some dissolved metals and some micro organisms. Special filters can be used, or alum can be added to the water.

Alum (aluminium potassium sulfate) is used in the food industry (pickling powder) and is non toxic. Add a pinch of alum per 4 litres of water (more if necessary). Mix well. Stir occasionally for 30 minutes, then allow 30-60 minutes to settle. Decant or pour through a paper filter to remove debris.

Step 2. Iodine Tablets: These tablets will remain active for six months after opening, provided the bottle remains capped. (It is a good idea to write 'Expires:' and the date six months hence on the bottle when you open it.) Iodine tablets must be stored away from excess heat or moisture. The purifying effect of iodine depends on the temperature of the water you are treating. e.g. for Potable Aqua™ - add one iodine tablet to one litre of water and leave to stand as follows:

water temperature	5°C	15°C	30°C
time (minutes)	60	30	15

Step 3. To make treated water taste better *after disinfection time is complete*, you may add a pinch of vitamin C powder or the usual quantity of drink flavouring.

Commercially produced water filters/purifiers

Due to the rigmarole above, commercially produced water purifiers (e.g. PentaPure™ or PUR™ products) are popular for long trips. Different models and sizes are available to purify even the most heavily contaminated water. They incorporate filters, iodine and de-tasting agents. They work quickly, the water tastes fine and they are more environmentally sound (fewer plastic bottles, and heating costs). Unfortunately there is a higher up front cost.

Container

Be careful not to place clean water in a contaminated container. Drink out of clean cups. Carry some straws.

Drinking water and avoiding dehydration

Dehydration is a very common problem among travellers. It is easy to get dehydrated in tropical countries where the weather is hot and the water is unsafe.

If you wait until you are thirsty, it is too late.

The best way to ensure you *do* drink plenty of water is to always have safe water on hand. The following hint may be helpful. Every morning *buy or treat one or two large bottles of water and put them in your day pack or bag.* If the water is easily accessible you will drink more. Plus, nobody wants to carry several kilograms of water around all day. The weight of the water is an incentive and reminder to drink more water.

Clues to pick a safe restaurant

The safest option:

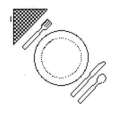

Of course there is no guarantee, but it is unusual to get food poisoning or other diseases if eating in five star hotels or popular tourist restaurants. These establishments have an economic need to maintain a high standard.

If you are backpacking

In many developing countries there are no Government Health Inspectors. It's up to you. There are clues which will help you pick authentic *and* hygienic restaurants to try the local delicacies. Ask yourself the following questions.

1. How clean is the kitchen?

Can you see the food being prepared? Ideally you want a restaurant with:

Screens to keep the insects out

Guaranteed refrigeration facilities

Careful food preparation

- vegetables washed in chemical solution
- workers with clean hands
- attention to proper hygiene
- ice made from clean water

2. How clean is the eating area?

Are the tables clean? Is the cutlery clean? Are flies abundant? Are the staff wiping dishes, tables and everything else with the one cloth? Atmosphere is one thing, but be suspicious when it leans too far toward dingy and dirty.

3. Are the toilets clean?

4. What is the reputation?

Is this restaurant popular with tour guides, tourists, expatriates? Do you know others who have eaten there safely? Be a little cautious about locals' recommendations. Local haunts may be safe for locals. Newly arrived travellers, however, may become quite sick from 'authentic' local germs. Accustom yourself to local food gradually. Start with small meals, mild curries and work up.

Street Stalls

Choose busy street stalls. The food is consumed quickly. It's probably good too!

ACCIDENTS

Medical care may be difficult to obtain in developing countries and small injuries may get complications and turn into serious medical problems. Even so called 'minor' injuries such as a sprained ankle will severely restrict your holiday.

More travellers die from accidents than any other medical problem while away. The most common cause of serious injury is car or bike crashes.

Most accidents are avoidable. Travelling means doing different things of course - even taking a few risks. However, these risks must be balanced with the risk of injury. Don't let your safety standards drop just because you are away from home. 'The Price of Life is Eternal Vigilance'.

Sightseeing hazards

Watch your step
This is especially important if you have weak ankles. Ruins are often strewn with rocks and potholes. Canal embankments may have ropes along the ground to tie up boats. Don't keep walking backwards to get that ultimate photo. This sounds obvious, but a tourist died in Australia recently from falling off a cliff under these circumstances!

Remove your sunglasses
Tombs, caves or temples are often poorly lit. Your eyes will take time to adjust to the light. These 'attractions' often have unexpectedly low ceilings or uneven floors.

Backpackers accommodation safety

1. Check the fire escape
Know where it is. Make sure it is not obstructed. Keep a torch by your bed. Plan how you would escape if necessary. In a smoke-filled room there is more oxygen if you crawl along the floor.

2. Beware of Balconies
Every year travellers die or suffer serious injury from falls off balconies. The floor of the balcony may be designed to look pretty but can be very slippery. Check the balustrade fixing is sound. It also needs to be sufficiently high to stop you overbalancing and falling. If not - stay well clear!

3. Bathrooms
The world has an astonishing array of different shower fittings. The water may be hotter than you expect. Turn the shower on *before* you get in. Watch out for steps around bathtubs or showers. These become especially hazardous if you are trying to escape a spray of unexpectedly hot water. Bathroom floors can be very slippery. In Spanish speaking countries the 'C' on the tap stands for 'calliente' or hot. In France the 'C' means 'chaud' also translating as hot.

Motorbike Safety

Avoid Motorbikes
Accidents on (or off) motorbikes are extremely common among travellers. For example the Koh Samui Hospital in Thailand sees nine people a day with motor bike injuries! If you don't ride them at home, it's safer to avoid them while you are away.

Wear a helmet
If you ride motorbikes, you need the right gear - helmets are essential. Open shoes, bare arms or legs will give no protection from a nasty gravel rash if you have an accident.

Hire a sound machine
Maintenance of engines and equipment may be extremely casual in developing countries. Rust is more aggressive in the tropics. Check the brakes.

Tuk Tuk
The 'Tuk Tuk' is a three wheeled vehicle in common use in Asia and India. It looks like a motorbike on steroids. Limit your use of these – if the smog doesn't kill you, an accident will.

Car safety

Motor vehicle accidents are the most common cause of death in travellers. Fatigue, lack of seat belt use, unfamiliar conditions such as driving on the 'other side of the road', and alcohol are common factors causing road crashes among tourists. Medical care in the event of a crash may be unavailable or even make the injuries worse.

The local drivers have their own unwritten road rules (?seem like skilled maniacs). In some parts of the world, dangerous overtaking has been elevated to an art form. Even if the roads are good, they are filled with many large trucks, buses, motor bikes, cars and careless pedestrians.

Choose the safest vehicle

Cars are proven to be safer than motorbikes. Open trucks and overloaded buses may be hazardous to your health.

If driving yourself, rent a bigger car. If possible choose one with seatbelts, (including child restraints if relevant,) and airbags. If possible, request automatic transmission so there is less to distract you while driving in unfamiliar surroundings. Rent from a reliable company. Check the spare tyre. Find out who to call if the car breaks down.

"Belt up"

In many countries it is not compulsory however you may not be covered by insurance if you fail to wear a seatbelt.

Stay sober when driving

No matter where you are, or who you are, alcohol is the single most deadly contributing factor to road accidents. If you drink, don't drive, and try to ensure you are not a passenger when the driver has been drinking.

Don't drive if tired

Fatigue or jetlag *plus* unfamiliar roads and driving conditions make a deadly combination. Wait one day to get acclimatised before you get behind a wheel. Seek local advice regarding realistic travelling times. Take regular rest stops during long drives. Get out and stretch your legs. Have meal breaks - hungry drivers have slower reaction times. Driving in daylight is much safer - accidents are more common at night.

Don't speed

Drive according to the road conditions. Stick to the speed limits and follow the road rules, even if they are not reliably enforced in that country.

Car safety continued

Beware of animals

Whether they are kangaroos, cows, moose, camels, or bears, collisions will make a mess of you, your car (and them.) Every year in the USA 10,000 people are injured and over 100 are killed in collisions with animals. Be especially careful at dusk in isolated areas.

Driving on the 'wrong' side of the road

If you are driving in a country where they use the 'other' side of the road to what you are used to, your risk of an accident is greatly increased.

It is easy when you are on a big highway to stay on the correct side of the road. It is also easy to *forget* and turn the *wrong* way when entering the road from a driveway, making turns onto a deserted road or when driving in busy traffic. Confusion over which side of the road to drive on was reported to be a major factor in the death of an American tourist in Brisbane recently.

Each time you go round a corner remind yourself out loud - Turn *left onto the right hand side of the road.* (or right onto the left hand side of the road depending on where you are). This will help get you into the new habit.

Pedestrian safety

Look both ways.
In countries where they drive on the 'other' side of the road to what you are used to, cars *sneak up on* you unexpectedly from the 'wrong' direction. Be aware this is a very common cause of pedestrian accidents in travellers.

Also be careful crossing roads at dusk. It may be difficult to judge how fast a car is approaching, especially if it is speeding.

Aeroplane safety

Choose the airline with the best safety record. Yes, the unexpected can always happen and even the concorde can blow up. However it really is *safer* to travel with a reputable airline than to drive a car. It is lack of familiarity with air travel that makes many people worry about flying. Once you are in the air, the most important thing you can do from a safety point of view is to keep your seatbelt fastened when the seat belts sign is illuminated.

SEX AND DISEASE

There is a wide range of sexually transmitted diseases including AIDS, Hepatitis B, Genital warts, Herpes, Gonorrhoea, Syphilis, Chancroid, and others. AIDS is the most serious.

Some of these diseases are resistant to standard antibiotics, especially in Asia.

Travellers are more at risk!

People are estimated to be 200 times more likely to contract AIDS while travelling, than when at home. The reasons for this increased risk are thought to be:

1. A change in behaviour when away from home. Travellers are more likely to engage in sexual activity with different partners e.g. fellow travellers or local sex workers.

2. Travellers often visit countries where the incidence of AIDS or other sexually transmitted diseases is higher than in their own country.

To Decrease Your Risks

1. Practice Safe Sex

Safe sex means not exchanging semen, blood or vaginal fluids with your partner. Whenever you engage in intercourse, you should use a condom. It should be used according to the instructions provided by the manufacturer. If lubricant is needed it must be water soluble e.g. KY, Wetstuff, Lubafax. Buy your condoms before you go. Locally made condoms may be of poor quality and break when used. They may also be the wrong size. e.g condoms in Asia are reported to be smaller than westerners require.

2. Avoid sexual contact

Reducing the number of sexual partners reduces your risk.

3. Beware of alcohol

Despite the *best* intentions, many unsafe contacts occur when a person's judgement is affected by drugs or alcohol. It may only take one unsafe sexual contact to pass on the AIDS virus.

4. Also avoid

Blood transfusions, injections (unless using your own sterile equipment), dental procedures, ear piercing, acupuncture, tattooing, manicures, shaving by public barbers, sharing razors or toothbrushes.

MIND ALTERING DRUGS

People are more likely to experiment with "mind altering drugs" while travelling.

Travellers are away from the usual social restraints such as family and friends, and they don't have to get up and go to work the next day. They are generally more relaxed and in 'holiday mode'. Many people see alcohol as an integral part of the holiday experience.

Alcohol
Alcohol is often very cheap and readily available overseas. It is worth checking the alcoholic content of what you are drinking. The brews overseas often have a higher alcoholic content than you may be used to, e.g. some varieties of Mekong whisky would be a good substitute for rocket fuel.

Additives or contaminants in the alcohol may be different and lead to unusually severe hangovers.

Illegal drugs
Experimentation with these sorts of drugs is extremely dangerous to your health and not recommended (to say the least).

Drugs are cheaper, and more widely available in most developing countries. Intravenous drugs carry a risk of contracting diseases such as AIDS. Drugs may be stronger or laced with harmful contaminants. There is often no-one to pick you up and take you home if you lose control. Accidents are more likely when 'under the influence'.

These sort of drugs are often still illegal and one can go to jail.

INSECT BITES

Why you need to be careful

Insect bites can hurt, but may also set off allergic reactions or become infected. Some insects are poisonous, e.g. spiders, and scorpions are very prevalent in some parts of the world. The most worrying thing is that some insects carry disease, e.g. Malaria, Yellow Fever, Dengue Fever, Japanese B Encephalitis, Filariasis, Kala Azar, Onchocerciasis, Typhus, Leishmaniasis, Sleeping sickness, Chagas' disease, Plague, Relapsing Fever, or Lyme Disease.

How to avoid insects

Ask the locals about the resident insect 'pests', especially spots to avoid, and the times of day they are bad. Choose accommodation with screens. Avoid mosquitoes as described on page 16. Mosquito bites are best avoided during the day as well as the evening. Day biting mosquitoes carry Dengue Fever. In Africa, try to avoid large (tsetse) flies. In areas where scorpions occur, check your shoes before putting them on. In tick or leech affected areas, always use repellents when bushwalking and check your body each night for 'hangers on'.

Sleeping

Check your bedding is clean. Head lice can be picked up from contaminated sheets. Insecticide treated sleep sheets are available and a most effective way to minimise your contact with the bed bugs, lice or fleas which may be present in some low budget hotels. Never sleep inside mud (adobe) huts in the Americas.

It is important to protect yourself from mosquitoes even if you are sleeping during the day.

Treated bed nets are very effective. Sadly, sandflies can pass through ordinary mosquito nets.

RABIES

WHO ME??

Do not go near, pat or play with animals
Playing with animals cannot give you Rabies, but if you are *bitten, scratched or licked over broken skin*, then you could catch the virus from the animal's saliva. Being scratched by a paw is most unlikely to lead to infection. If you don't play with or go near animals, you usually won't get bitten.

Which animals carry Rabies?
The Rabies virus is present in most developing countries. Dogs are the main source of rabies in humans, but it can occur in any mammal. Be especially wary of dogs, cats, bats and monkeys. Even animals that have been vaccinated against Rabies can sometimes transmit the disease to people.

If in doubt and you are bitten by an animal – seek local medical advice.

Avoid bat caves. Persons have caught rabies by *inhaling* the virus whilst visiting bat caves, (contracting rabies in this way is very rare though).

Do the rabid animals look sick?
No, the animal may look normal - initially anyway. Animals with rabies may also behave unpredictably.

Children are at risk
Supervise children closely if they are near animals, they are particularly at risk. They are low to the ground, and fearless and hence may get bitten quite severely.

Joggers and cyclists
Think twice about jogging or cycling in rural areas. Cyclists in India are particularly at risk of being bitten.

If you get bitten
All animal bites or scratches should be treated as potentially rabies infected until proven otherwise. See page 101 for information on treatment of animal bites.

WORMS AND PARASITES

**Five easy ways to
avoid infestation**

1. Wash your hands frequently

Always wash your hands before eating and after using the
toilet. Contamination is all around – on money, shoelaces,
door handles.

2. Don't bite your nails

Beware of biting your nails. This habit will transfer germs
from your surroundings to your stomach.

3. Choose your food and fluids carefully.

If you follow the eating and drinking suggestions on pp 42-46,
you will dramatically reduce your contact with worms and
parasites as well as gastroenteritis.

4. Keep your shoes on

Almost one quarter of the world's population is infected with
hookworm. Hookworm larvae may be present in soil or sand.
These immature worms can enter your body through bare
skin while you are standing or sitting in contact with the
ground. Beach sand below the 'high tide mark' is washed
twice daily so it is safe to sit on. 'Closed in' shoes also provide
protection from snakes and sunburn. If you wear thongs or
other footwear in communal showers you will minimise the
chance of fungal infections and plantar warts. Bare feet are
fine in hotel rooms on carpet.

5. Avoid contact with still, fresh water

It is not recommended to swim, bathe, shower, or wade in
still, fresh water in areas infected with Schistosomiasis
(bilharzia). Salt or chlorinated water is safe.

The parasite is present in parts of Africa (especially Lake
Malawi and Lake Kariba), South America, and Asia. Use hip
waders, waterproof boots and/or gloves if wading streams or
collecting water. If swimming is unavoidable, apply DEET
containing repellent to your skin before water contact. After
swimming, towel dry vigorously and apply rubbing alcohol
(methylated spirits or even cheap Scotch) to the skin. These
measures will help deter the larval worms from hitching a
ride.(See pages 141-143 for details, including a map of
affected countries.)

HOT CLIMATES

Who is most at risk of heat stress?
No-one is immune if it is hot enough. However, if you are young, physically fit and relatively thin, you will adapt to hot climates more quickly. The sweat glands will learn to start up more quickly, increase sweat production and conserve salt. The process of adaptation takes about two weeks. If you are over 65, overweight or have heart or blood pressure problems, you will probably 'feel the heat' more. Some individuals are genetically more prone to over-heating and illness increases your risk of over-heating.

Everyone needs an awareness of avoiding heat stress, however if you are particularly susceptible to the heat, extra care will be needed.

12 tips for preventing heat stress

1. Plan to avoid the heat if possible
Avoid long periods of time directly in the hot sun. Plan your day so you do not go out in the heat of the day. (As the saying goes ...*mad dogs and Englishmen go out in the midday sun.*) Try to avoid undue exertion in the heat. However it is interesting to note that those who exercise in the heat will adapt to the heat a little more quickly.

2. Wear loose cotton clothes
Long pants and long sleeves are cooler than shorts and short sleeves. *Light* coloured clothes are better, since they reflect the heat. (The Arabs in their long white robes have the right idea.)

3. Wear covered shoes
They should be made from a breathable material and cover the foot. Sandals do not protect feet from sunburn.

4. Don't forget a hat!
Sunshine on a beach and near the water is especially deceptive. Ideally the hat should have a wide brim and shade the neck.

5. Wear sunglasses
Prolonged exposure to glare will damage your eyes.

6. Drink more liquids

Make sure you always have access to clean water so you are not tempted to drink the local variety which may be contaminated. In the tropics, your thirst sensation is <u>not</u> reliable! You need to drink fluid a little *beyond* the point of thirst quenching or you will become dehydrated. If you are drinking enough fluid, your urine will be consistently pale.

7. Avoid excessive caffeine

Coffee, tea and caffeinated drinks will make dehydration worse, as will alcohol. If you are thirsty - you need water.

8. Eat lightly

You will feel better if you stick to fruit and vegetables. Avoid salads if they are not hygienically prepared.

9. Salt?

A little extra salt in your food or drinks will offset the increased losses from sweating. Most people have adequate salt in their diet so salt tablets are not recommended. If you have heart or blood pressure problems you should consult your doctor regarding salt intake.

10. Beware of humidity

In dry climates, sweat is able to evaporate and remove heat from the body. In humid environments, the sweat on your skin cannot evaporate because the air is *already* full of water. Heat cannot escape, and overheating occurs rapidly. Under these conditions, exert yourself as little as possible.

11. Retreat to air conditioning

Air-conditioned environments such as hotels, or movie theatres are havens when you feel overheated.

12. Use Blockout 15+ regularly

For best effect, blockout should be applied 30 minutes before exposure. Avoid the sun especially between 10.00am and 2.00pm. Beware of cloudy days, or smoggy days. One traveller got quite sunburnt in Bangkok and remarked "I normally always wear blockout when I'm out in Australia, but the weather seemed so dull because of all the smog, I didn't think I needed it."

Dermatologists strongly advise against "sunbathing".

The suns rays *are* damaging to human skin; causing premature ageing, wrinkling, spotting and of course skin cancers. If you are determined to get a tan, remember it is a *gradual* process. Skin which tans after burning will peel off in three weeks.

COLD CLIMATES

5 hints to dressing warmly

1. Wear socks and gloves
Your fingers and toes are the most susceptible to frostbite. Good quality socks and gloves should be worn. Mittens are better if you are prone to cold fingers.

2. Always wear a hat or beanie
A great deal of body heat is lost from the head <u>and neck</u> especially while sleeping and at altitude. Always wear a head covering (preferably a wool beanie) to keep your head warm, and a scarf, muff or balaclava to keep your neck warm. Keep your ears covered as they are susceptible to frostbite.

3. Avoid wearing shorts
A high wind chill factor on your bare legs can lead to hypothermia very quickly. Long trousers will prevent this.

4. Dress in layers
Layers trap air which keeps you warm. Dressing in multiple thin layers provides flexibility. Layers can be removed if you become more active or the weather warms up. The layer closest to the body needs to keep the skin dry by sucking sweat away e.g. polypropylene. Middle layers need to provide insulation and yet breathe e.g. fleece fabric.

5. Windproof clothing on top
The top layer needs to be waterproof and windproof, and yet allow sweat to escape. Goretex™ and similar fabrics do this - the pore size stops liquid water but allows water vapour to pass.

Eating in cold climates
Frequent small meals has been shown to provide the best energy levels in cold climates. Your body needs plenty of fuel to produce heat. Skipping meals in cold climates is not 'an easy way to shed pounds'. Lack of food will make you tired and more susceptible to frostbite, hypothermia and injuries.

Drinking Liquids
Drink plenty of liquids, especially water. In cold environments you are less aware of losing moisture from your body. Cold air is very dry and draws moisture from the skin and lungs as you breathe. Slight dehydration *can* make a big difference. Studies on world class skiers show a mere 2% reduction in body fluids may reduce performance up to 15%. Note that alcohol will not warm you up if you are seriously cold – you just won't care that you are cold.

WOMEN TRAVELLERS

Feminine hygiene

Toilets in some parts of the world *can* be extremely unclean. During a menstrual period, ensure your hands are clean before tampons are used. Wash hands with soap and water (tap water is OK) and dry with a clean towel. Products such as Microshield™ hand wash can be used where soap and water is not available. The use of tampon applicators may be convenient.

Travelling and the Pill

Delaying Periods ....and the Pill

Some contraceptive pills can be taken continuously, thus avoiding periods altogether. This is safe. It is easier with monophasic (one strength pills) like Microgynon, Levlen, or Nordette. You simply skip the sugar pills for that month. This will delay your period 3 weeks. You can usually skip three periods in a row without any worries at all.

If you are taking 'multiple dose pills' (e.g. Triquilar, Triphasil), skipping the sugar pills may not work. To delay a period on these pills you need to do this: when you reach the end of your active pills for the month - instead of taking the sugar pills, use a spare packet and take the last week of active pills from the spare packet. Then take the sugar pills. This will delay your period for a week.

Always take a 'Saturday' pill on a Saturday or confusion may occur. Discuss this with your doctor. If you want to skip periods, it may be easier to temporarily change to a 'one strength pill'.

Time Zones....and the Pill

This is not important for nearby destinations e.g. Singapore, but may be important for the UK or the United States. Spotting, irregular periods, or even pregnancy may occur if you delay or miss pills. Keep a watch on home time so that while overseas you continue to take your pill at your usual *home* time. This is the easiest way.

If the pill-taking-time works out to be the middle of the night, adjust it by about four hours *earlier or later* each day until you get to a suitable local time. If in doubt, always take your pill earlier rather than later.

Vomiting ....and the Pill
If you vomit within five hours of taking the pill it may not have been absorbed. You should take another pill to replace the one lost.

Diarrhoea ....and the Pill
It is difficult to predict the effect that diarrhoea will have on pill absorption. The safest course of action is to continue taking the pill, but use other means of contraception while you have severe diarrhoea and until 14 days after the severe diarrhoea has ceased.

Antibiotics ....and the Pill
This is important if you need to take antibiotics for diarrhoea. Some antibiotics interfere with the effectiveness of the contraceptive pill. This may lead to spotting in the middle of the month, or even pregnancy. For absolute safety from pregnancy - use other means of contraception while taking the antibiotic and for 14 days after.

Malaria tablets ...and the Pill
Chloroquine, Maloprim, and mefloquine (Lariam) do not interfere with the oral contraceptive pill. Doxycycline may interfere with the contraceptive pill leading to irregular bleeding or even pregnancy. Use other means of contraception while on doxycycline.

High altitude ....and the Pill
If your trip spends less than four weeks at high altitudes, it is safe to continue taking your pill. (Most treks in Nepal fall into this category.) You may need to cease the pill if you will be travelling *above 3,700 metres* for *more than 4 weeks* . There is a small increased risk of blood clots in the brain, lungs, or legs. The blood 'thickens' at high altitudes, in order to carry oxygen more efficiently. The pill also causes 'thickening' to a small extent. The combination of both may be harmful. Women planning a trip like this may need to stop the pill several weeks before they travel, particularly if they smoke. Discuss this with the doctor.

Carry spare packets
It is vital you carry spare packets. If you lose any pills through vomiting or diarrhoea, it is better to use a replacement pill for the correct day of the week, i.e. take a Thursday pill on a Thursday.

Other female concerns

Irregular periods

If you are not on the pill, it is common to have irregular periods while travelling, especially on long and/or busy or stressful trips. It is often due to the upset in routine. It is harmless except for the worry of possible pregnancy.

Thrush

A most unpleasant condition to have while travelling! Avoid unnecessary antibiotics, try not to get 'rundown', pay careful attention to hygiene, wear cotton underclothes, and treat thrush promptly if symptoms develop (see page 111).

Cystitis/Urinary Tract Infection

Drink more fluids! Cystitis may be partly due to a poor fluid intake. Many women experience cystitis or urinary tract infections when travelling. If you are prone to this, ensure you drink plenty of fluids, and treat yourself promptly if symptoms develop, see page110.

Emergency Contraception

Plan ahead so you don't need it, but if you do, see page 111.

Women travelling in Arab countries

Different Customs

Customs are very strict in 'devout' countries. There is a great contrast between the dress and behaviour of the average western woman, and that of the local women. In these countries, this contrast has furthered the mistaken belief that 'western women' are promiscuous. Find out all you can about the customs and respect them.

Dress modestly

It is best not to invite danger. Always try to dress with complete modesty by local standards. Respect for a woman decreases with the amount of skin she has showing. In some cases even the shape of various parts of the body (e.g. tight jeans) is considered offensive. A long, loose skirt and long sleeved shirt with high neck, is usually safe. Dark sunglasses are useful if you wish to avoid eye contact with the locals.

Travel in a group

In these countries, travelling in a group may be a great help.

Personal Security

Even at home, your personal security can never be taken for granted. Whenever you travel overseas, a few extra precautions will ensure your personal safety. Both sexes are at risk. It is important to keep someone at home regularly informed of your movements.

Leave expensive trappings at home
Expensive watches, rings, earrings, necklaces, handbags, purses, even expensive clothes attract criminals like moths to a flame - let someone else attract the 'moths'.

Keep your hands free
Interviews with criminals in prison revealed they target 'vulnerable' looking men and women in a hurry, encumbered by purses, and packages. It is better to venture out with no bag at all. Possessions can be tucked onto your person in pockets, or money belts etc. If a bag is absolutely necessary, a battered backpack will keep your hands free. Walking around with headphones in your ears also makes you vulnerable.

Plan ahead
If travelling independently, research the places you are going to visit so you know the parts of town to avoid and do not stand around looking lost in train or bus stations. Being in a hurry puts your personal security at greater risk. There is less time to look around and spot dangers. Keep yourself out of *potentially* dangerous situations. Be a little suspicious. There are very poor and desperate people around. Stick to public places such as restaurants for meeting persons you do not know well. Hitchhiking is akin to playing Russian roulette.

Have a decoy ready
Carry a money clip containing a $50 note in an accessible pocket. If you get held up, you can throw the weighted note at the bandit and run the other way. The weight of the money clip stops the note blowing back at you.

Drink spiking
Only drink something you have opened and poured yourself. Sadly, there are drugs such as Rohypnol which are tasteless, and which have been slipped into drinks by unscrupulous types, and travellers have woken up robbed or raped.

Hand to hand self defense
Training in this type of self defense is a good idea before departure for some travellers. It could save your life.

TRAVELLING WITH CHILDREN

The usual 'travelling well' precautions apply with a few extras.

While travelling

Infants may need to breast feed or take a bottle as the aeroplane takes off and lands. Swallowing helps the pressure in their ears equalise, and minimises ear pain. Older children may find it helpful to suck a lolly. Some children are prone to motion sickness, especially if they read or do puzzles during long car journeys. Carry a basin (or vomit bag from the plane) in the car just in case.

Eating and Drinking

The food and water precautions previously outlined are particularly important. Children under 3 years of age tend to get diarrhoea which is more severe and lasts longer. As much as possible, watch what they eat and don't allow children to drink untreated water. Carry a wet washer, or antiseptic hand wash so you can clean their hands regularly. Try to regularly sterilise the utensils they use such as bottles, cups etc. Always use treated water for drinking, cleaning their teeth and washing toothbrushes. Discourage them from drinking bath water.

Hot and cold climates

Be careful to protect children from extremes of heat or cold. Beware of frostbite on tiny fingers and toes. Children cannot regulate their body temperature as well as adults. Dress them appropriately and offer fluids regularly. Children can dehydrate rapidly and their thirst sensation is unreliable. Use maximum sunscreen to protect their delicate skin.

Accidents

While travelling, you have less control over a child's environment. Drownings, poisonings, burns, and falls are particular hazards. Watch out for unfenced pools and waterways – (a one year old Australian baby recently drowned in Indonesia). Closely supervise children around animals. Make sure you keep medications out of their reach e.g. locked in your suitcase.

HIGH ALTITUDE TRAVELLERS

8848	Everest
5895	Kilimanjaro
5500	Everest Base camp
4101	Kinabalu
3577	La Paz
2800	Machu Pichu
2300	Mexico city
2230	Kosciusko
867	Uluru (Ayers Rock)
0	Sea level

What is Altitude Sickness?

The air is 'thinner' as altitude increases. Altitude sickness is a group of unpleasant symptoms which start 6-48 hours after rapid ascent to high altitude. They are due to the lack of available oxygen in the gut, muscles, brain, lungs etc. Individual susceptibility depends on how high you go, how fast you get there, and your genetic makeup. No one is immune. Physically fit persons suffer more if they climb faster.

How high is high ?

Altitude sickness is rare below 2,500 metres. A study in the Swiss Alps demonstrated as follows -

Height in metres above sea level	% of climbers with Altitude Sickness
2850 m	9%
3650 m	34%
4559m	53%

Symptoms of Altitude Sickness

MILD	SEVERE †
Headache	Severe headache
Nausea	Unsteadiness on feet
Lack of appetite	Unusual behaviour
Unusual tiredness	Extreme drowsiness
Trouble sleeping	Difficulty breathing
Shivering	Blue nails and lips
Unusual breathing in sleep*	Cough with frothy sputum

* If you listen to your fellow travellers while they are asleep at altitude, it is normal for their breathing to sound patchy; very deep breathing followed by a short period when they stop breathing. It is best not to wake them to see if they are OK.

† Severe Altitude Sickness comes in two varieties – fluid on the brain known as HACE – High Altitude Cerebral Edema (American spelling) – and fluid on the lung known as HAPE - High Altitude Pulmonary Edema. Both 'severe' varieties kill unprepared travellers and climbers every year.

8 Steps to minimising altitude sickness

1. Plan your itinerary
Go up slowly. A rough guideline is to ascend *no more than 300 metres per day* when you are over 3,000 metres.

2. Consider using Diamox
If a rapid ascent is necessary, or you have suffered altitude sickness before, your travel doctor may advise acetazolamide = Diamox (a prescription medication). Diamox will prevent mild symptoms such as the altitude headache, and speed up your adaptation to altitude. (It will not mask your symptoms of altitude sickness, while you get steadily worse without realising it.) The mechanism of action is not exactly known, but it is thought to change how you process carbon dioxide in the kidneys. To take it for prevention, start two days before you reach 2700m. **Take half a tablet (=125mg) morning and night.** It is not recommended if you are allergic to sulphur drugs. It may cause tingling sensation in your hands and feet, and make carbonated drinks (including beer) taste funny. Most people only use them for four days in total, but the tablets can be continued for up to two weeks.

3. Get enough rest
Take it easy, your heart works harder at altitude. Rest for 24 hours if you fly directly from sea level to high altitude cities e.g. Cusco, Quito, Mexico City.

4. Eat light meals
Eat light, starchy meals rather than fatty ones. Try to avoid very salty food. (Peruvians like their food quite salty.)

5. Drink more fluid
Mountain air is dry. Dehydration will make altitude sickness worse. Aim for 6 to 8 litres per day, so your urine is pale. Coca tea is a popular remedy in the Andes - an acquired taste (to say the least!). For best effect have 3-4 cups per day using the tea with real coca leaves in boiling water.

6. Avoid alcohol/cigarettes especially on first day
Alcohol increases dehydration, and depresses breathing. One *standard drink* per day is usually safe after the first day. Smoking decreases your available oxygen even further.

7. Avoid sleeping pills
Insomnia at altitude is due to oxygen starvation. Sedatives may slow your breathing and make the symptoms worse.

8. Treat any infection quickly
Infection increases oxygen needs. Treat infection (e.g. wound infection, bronchitis, diarrhoea) sooner rather than later.

Treatment of Altitude Sickness

If symptoms are mild.
Do not sleep at higher altitudes until you feel better. During rest days, it is okay to climb to higher altitudes but descend to sleep. Diamox (125mg twice a day) may be used to *treat* mild symptoms of altitude sickness. Even if you are already taking Diamox for prevention, you can take an extra 250 mg tablet once for treatment. For example if you are visiting Cusco and wake during the first night with symptoms – take one 250mg Diamox (plus ibuprofen, panadol or aspirin) to treat the headache, then continue with a half tablet (125mg) every 12 hours. Hotels may have oxygen on hand or call their doctor.

If symptoms are severe
There is no time to lose. *Descend!* 300 metres can make a huge difference. Even if it is the middle of the night, get the sufferer down. Be wary of unco-operative companions, who deny they are sick and refuse to descend. Change of personality may be a sign of severe altitude sickness. Do not wait for a helicopter. Use whatever transport is available. If they cannot walk or stagger, they need to be carried down by porter, yak or horse. Severe altitude sickness requires urgent, experienced medical help and constant supervision. A Gamow bag (portable hyperbaric chamber) may buy some time. Dexamethasone and nitrous oxide are not for self treatment.

Other problems at altitude

Swelling
Some people notice swelling of their body at altitude e.g. puffy eyes, face or hands in the morning and ankle swelling later in the day. They may feel swollen and well, or have associated symptoms of mild altitude sickness. It is not a serious problem. The fluid disappears when you descend.

Sunburn
Sunburn occurs rapidly as there is less atmosphere to filter the sun's rays. Sunscreen, hats, long sleeved clothing are essential.

Snow blindness
Polaroid or skier's sunglasses with side protection are best worn at all times. Unshielded glare at altitude will rapidly burn the back of your eye. Most people will not notice symptoms until they wake at night with gritty and very sore eyes.

Knee pain
When walking down hills, try to take the weight of the body with the leading leg a little bent at the knee. This will prevent the common problem of trekker's knee.

GOING TO THE SNOW

Snow Skiers

Gear
Keep your gear in good order and have it serviced yearly. Know how to check your own bindings. Check them daily while in the snow.

Sunglasses
If you ski without sunglasses you risk permanent damage to your eyes. Ultraviolet light is partly responsible for cataracts and other vision problems in the elderly. Over years of exposure it also causes permanent, ugly fat deposits (pinguecula) to build up on the white of your eye. Larger sunglasses are better as they will protect the delicate skin around your eyes. Side flanges will stop light sneaking around the sides of the lenses. Winter sunglasses should filter out all ultraviolet, and about 90% of visible light. Stand two feet from a mirror with sunglasses on and you should not be able to see your eyes.

Avoiding injuries
You can decrease your risk of injury if you:
* undertake pre season training
* check your bindings every day
* warm up before the first run, and after lunch
* take lessons
* endeavour to ski in control
* avoid alcohol during skiing
* stop when tired - the risk of injury is high during the last run of the day.
* maintain fluid and food intake
* stay within the patrolled areas unless you are prepared for an overnight stay in the snow.

If you do get hurt:
Cold minimises the swelling so an injury will feel deceptively minor. You will make the injury worse if you continue to ski. Don't ski until you get it checked by a doctor. This will ensure you do not lose any more precious skiing time than is absolutely necessary!!!

Snow Mobiles

Rent a reputable one.
Dress warmly as there is a high wind chill factor when moving at speed.
Wear sunglasses.
Children should wear ear plugs.
Stay on the trails – be aware of avalanche danger.
Slow down if inexperienced.

Toboggans

Stick to known toboggan runs. Tobogganists are more likely to be injured than snow skiers. Toboggans are difficult to steer and it is easy to lose control and crash into people, rocks etc.

Saunas

A sauna will cause your blood vessels to dilate. If you are dehydrated you will experience dizziness, a headache and a feeling of weakness. If you sauna alone beware of falling asleep.

Spas

Must be clean
Conjunctivitis and wound infections are common after a spa if it is not clean. Check the spa is properly cleaned. If you are not sure, have a shower afterwards and wash yourself with soap. Avoid spas if you have open cuts and abrasions. Keep your head out of the water.

Alcohol
Don't have too much. Drinking Alcohol while in a spa will rapidly 'go to your head'. Heat and alcohol both have a tendency to lower your blood pressure. The result is you will feel lightheaded and may faint, or slip as you exit the spa. It is very embarrassing to break your ankle on a ski holiday from falling over in the spa!

SCUBA DIVERS

Gear

Check the gear thoroughly. Before hiring equipment, seek recommendations from the locals. Be concerned if dive shop staff do not ask to see your 'card'. Some dive shops are notorious for 'bad air'.

Dive tables

Be generous with safety margins on the dive tables. The best dive spots are often in remote areas. It may be a long way to the nearest decompression chamber!

Safety first

Do not be tempted to dive beyond your ability because someone will let you. It could be fatal. 20 out of 51 sports-diving deaths in Australia between 1980 and 1986 involved divers who were not properly trained for the dives which killed them. Only two deaths were triggered by equipment faults. Get a copy of the waterproof book, 'The Diving Emergency Handbook' by Lippmann and Bugg. Carry it in your dive bag. In the Australasian area there is a free emergency 24 hour phone number to access medical advice on possible diving-related illness; 1800 088 200.

Don't dive if sick

Accidents happen more commonly if you dive when feeling ill or generally weak. Do not dive with a severe cold. Decongestants such as pseudoephedrine, should be used with extreme caution. They *cannot* unblock a really clogged nose and you will not be able to 'equalise' underwater. They are useful for mild congestion, but they do wear off.

Don't drink and dive

Alcohol causes <u>diving</u> accidents like it causes <u>driving</u> accidents. Other drugs which impair concentration should also be avoided. Smoking prior to a dive decreases the amount of oxygen your blood can carry.

MOTION SICKNESS

What is it?

Motion sickness is a normal reaction to certain types of motion. The causes are varied and the syndrome is named accordingly; airsickness, seasickness, carsickness. Regardless of the cause, the end result is the same dreadful business; paleness, yawning, restlessness, clammy skin or cold sweat, excessive salivation, nausea, and vomiting.

Susceptibility

About one third of the population is highly susceptible, one third react only to fairly rough conditions, and the final third will become sick only under extreme conditions. Women are more susceptible than men. Persons 2-12 years are most susceptible with their susceptibility decreasing with age. Motion sickness is uncommon after age 50.

History

Motion sickness has plagued man since he began using vehicles to transport himself around. Cicero, Julius Caesar, Admiral Lord Nelson were notably susceptible. Even Lawrence of Arabia suffered from motion sickness when he was riding his camel during the desert campaign against the Turks. Until the 1940's it was believed that anyone who experienced motion sickness lacked 'moral fibre'.

Prevention of motion sickness?

The only truly effective method of prevention is totally impractical ..walk everywhere??? Continuous exposure to a particular motion usually means the symptoms subside within 3 days, although there are a few unfortunate souls who remain sensitive to it throughout prolonged exposure. Occasionally, after getting used to the motion, symptoms return when the motion stops e.g. you get off the ship.

Position yourself

The least irritating places are the front seat of a car where you can watch the road, amidships on a boat especially on a lower deck (or for short periods; in the swimming pool) or over the wing of an aircraft.
* lie down if possible
* get fresh air
* avoid strong odours, spicy or greasy foods
* never watch someone who is vomiting

Medications for the prevention of motion sickness

For maximum effect, you need to start the medicines *before* symptoms develop. Avoid alcohol as it can interact with motion sickness medication and/or make motion sickness worse. Adult doses are given below; for children's doses see drug reference table on pages 116-123.

Natural alternatives

Ginger has been found to be effective for some people. Ginger based tablets are available from health food shops. The dose of ginger required is somewhat uncertain.

For short trips (<8 hours)

Hyoscine tablets (Kwells 0.3mg) 1-2 tabs should be taken 30 minutes before travel. It acts for about 4 hours. Repeat in 4-6 hours if necessary but for longer trips see below.

For longer trips (> 8 hours)

i) Scopolamine (SCOP 1.5mg) patch is a tiny medicated 'spot'. One is stuck behind your ear, 6-8 hours before exposure to the motion. It is worn for three days; e.g. the first three days of boat trip.

NB SCOP and Kwells may cause dry mouth, blurry vision and dizziness. Occasionally SCOP can cause confusion especially if over 65yrs.

ii) Dimenhydrinate (Drammamine 50mg) One tab 3-4 times a day should be started 2 hours before travel. It can cause drowsiness and dizziness so do not use when driving.

iii) Promethazine (Avomine or Phenergan 25mg) is effective. Dose is one tablet each night, starting the night before travel. If necessary for shorter trips, take 2 hours before departure, however marked drowsiness is likely to develop.

Things which don't work so well

Prochlorperazine (Stemetil) is a common antinausea pill but is not so effective against motion sickness. Products that press on an acupuncture point in the wrist have shown no effect in clinical trials. Caffeine alone doesn't stop motion sickness but decreases the drowsiness caused by the pills.

If you are motion sick

Lie down. Close your eyes and avoid moving your head from side to side. If you are on deck and cannot lie down, try keeping your eyes fixed on the horizon. Avoid reading. Take slow deep breaths. Apply an icepack or cold cloth to your forehead and back of your neck. Small sips of non carbonated (flat) drinks, especially water or Gastrolyte solution will help replace fluids lost through vomiting.

If all else fails

The ship's doctor can usually give you an injection.

CULTURE SHOCK

What is Culture Shock?

Culture Shock is the temporary inability to cope with a different culture. Culture Shock can be felt with varying degrees of severity. When symptoms are mild, it may be described as Culture Fatigue. Reverse Culture Shock can also develop on return to one's home country after an extended stay away.

Who is most at risk?

Culture Shock is most common in people going to live and work overseas for several years, even to English-speaking countries.

Long term, budget travellers, visiting multiple countries may also experience it to varying degrees. Those travelling by themselves and/or in countries where they do not speak the language, are particularly at risk. When couples move overseas, the non-working partner often suffers culture shock more intensely. They do not have a familiar work environment, and work mates to cushion the impact. They also tend to be the one out in the 'thick of it' while trying to do the shopping, work out the transport system etc.

What causes Culture Shock?

Culture Shock is due to an excess of novelty.

Many of the rules you learned in childhood about how things work and how people behave suddenly change. In a different country there are many new things to get used to and worry about e.g. time zone shifts, differences in weather, food, language, money, tipping, taxes. Worries about avoiding illness, mugging, being ripped off, leaving things behind. Bus, train and air timetables take some figuring out. You often have to worry about where to stay, what to see, how much money this is all costing, and how important it is to have a good time. There are new people to meet, and new cultures and customs to understand. Each of the changes by themselves is a small challenge and part of the adventure of travel. If they occur simultaneously, it is possible to become overloaded - which leads to stress.

Furthermore, all this change and stress occurs in the absence of the usual social support system of family and friends.

Preparation for departure is usually a major undertaking and involves leaving your job, perhaps training your replacement, selling the car and/or house, putting possessions into storage, organising finances, passports, visas, saying goodbye to all the relatives and friends etc. Often you arrive in the new country feeling exhausted and in need of a holiday; but instead you are called on to deal with a dazzling array of new things.

Three stages of adaptation to a new culture

Note that different members of a family may go through the stages at different times.

1. Excitement

Initially there is great excitement at being away, out of the rut, seeing the world, meeting new people.

2. Disappointment

After the initial excitement of being away from home has settled, it is not unusual to feel lonely. You may also feel extremely disappointed that the experience is 'not what it was cracked up to be'.

Other symptoms commonly described are feeling anxious, depressed, tired, lacking in enthusiasm, bored, sleepy, homesick, or emotionally on the edge. You may get cravings for 'normal' food or 'normal' behaviour. Culture Shock may lead to unexplained crying. You may even decide you want to go home, and start fantasising about arriving home, explaining your behaviour to your friends etc.

This is all fairly normal.

Culture shock can even make you sick. Stress can weaken your immune system and increase your susceptibility to diseases such as diarrhoea or the flu. If it is very severe, Culture Shock can make you pack your bags and head home.

3. Adjustment

During this stage, the excess of novelty is under control. You can enjoy the new challenges and the new culture. There is excitement of a different sort.

So how do you make the transition from Disappointment to Adjustment? It takes time and patience. Some ways to assist the process are listed in the following section. (Incidentally, if you are returning home after a long time overseas, it can take quite some time to adjust back; this is known as Reverse Culture Shock and the hints to follow are relevant for those symptoms as well.)

Seven Ways to deal with Culture Shock

1. Be aware of it
Awareness and acceptance is the first and most important step. It is *normal* to feel overwhelmed in such circumstances.

2. Get used to things gradually
Don't expect to see too much or do too much all at once. Give yourself time e.g. months to get used to the many changes. Be patient.

3. Find yourself someone who knows the system
Other expatriates are a valuable source of information and moral support. They will help guide you through 'the system' most efficiently. They will be able to give you advice on where to shop, who gives a good haircut etc.

4. Have a disaster plan
It is comforting to know where to find reliable help if you need medical advice urgently. Do a test run of the emergency procedures. Ring the insurance or assistance company. Know where to go, and if necessary, drive the road you would take. If possible introduce yourself to the doctor, and let them know of any important medical history you may have such as allergies, medication etc. Find out the doctor's hours, alternative arrangements if you get sick in the middle of the night, or injured on the weekend, find out how they charge. While you are there, you might want to arrange medical checkups for any employees you have (e.g. for Tuberculosis) – the healthier they are, the better it is for you and them.

5. Take care of yourself
- Get plenty of rest.
- Eat as well as you can.
- Stay fit.
- Resist the temptation to drink a lot of alcohol
- Plan fun activities or even little holidays, so you can have a laugh and keep your sense of humour. In some postings shore leave is a necessity - not a luxury.

6. Keep in touch with friends / support network
'Phone Home', write letters, or email.

7. Try not to withdraw
Avoidance is a natural first response to the unknown. It is scary to learn new things, and painful to make mistakes. The normal tendency is to try and avoid this pain. If you do the thing you are afraid of, (within reason) you often find it is not as bad as you thought. If you learn some of the language you can interact more with the locals, and discover the great aspects of their culture.

IF YOU
GET SICK

TRAVELLERS FIRST AID

In this section the most common and most serious travellers health problems are discussed first. These instructions are not intended to replace a consultation with a competent doctor.

FINDING DOCTORS OVERSEAS

To find a reliable doctor in the place you are visiting, try the following:

1. Ring your Travel Insurance Hotline. They will usually be able to tell you the name of a reliable doctor nearby.

2. Go to an up-market hotel. Hotel doctors are usually reliable. Good hotels sometimes double as 'hospitals' in developing countries. Some hospitals provide only doctors. The nursing has to be done by family or friends. You may need to use your credit card, check into an up market hotel and use room service.

3. Ring your embassy The embassy staff will usually recommend a doctor. If there is no local embassy for your citizenship, one of the major English speaking embassies will usually be able to recommend a doctor e.g. US, Canadian, British, Australian, New Zealand.

If you cannot find a reliable doctor, it is important you look after yourself properly *until* you do. These Traveller's First Aid notes are written for a sick person to read and follow. If you are too sick to read the book and work out what is wrong then you definitely need to seek medical attention.

How to look up symptoms
To find directions for treatment of a particular condition, consult the table of contents on page 3. If your problem is not listed, try looking up 'SYMPTOMS' in the index at the back of this book for a list of common symptoms and the page reference for treatment.

The type of first aid involving mouth to mouth resuscitation, bandaging etc is well covered in general first aid books and is only briefly mentioned in this book under general emergencies. For travellers going to live 'in the middle of nowhere', the book 'Where There Is No Doctor' by D. Werner (Macmillan Press) will help you diagnose more serious things like appendicitis. For those travelling with children the book 'Your Child's Health Abroad' by Dr J Wilson-Howarth and Dr M Ellis (Bradt) is very useful.

8 KEYS FOR TREATING ANY ILLNESS

1. Rest !
Resting the whole body is good for the immune system. Stress is known to increase protein breakdown and interfere with the immune response. Even in the case of injury -resting the injured part is also important. For example don't walk on an injured leg - elevate the leg on pillows rather than hanging it down under a chair. This will decrease swelling and increase the blood flow to the limb which will further encourage healing.

2. Eat well
Eat healthy foods and drink plenty of fluids. The body needs nourishment to provide the building blocks of new tissues e.g. protein, vitamins (A, C and K), and trace elements (iron, zinc and copper). Try to minimise your consumption of alcohol and caffeine.

3. Don't smoke
Smoking slows healing by interfering with normal metabolism and decreasing the amount of oxygen carried by the blood.

4. Fever ? Think malaria
If you have visited a malarious country, don't forget that any fever could be malaria and you need to stop travelling and go and see a doctor as soon as possible.

5. Follow the instructions
Read the instructions, and follow them carefully. Do not give your tablets to others as they may be allergic to them. You may also need them later yourself.

6. Keep records
Keep a brief written record of any major symptoms e.g. fever or rash, what happened, date and time. Also record the date and dosage of any drugs you use for treatment. This will make it easier if you need to seek medical attention later.

7. Trust your body
You do have a powerful immune system. Give it a chance and you will usually recover. Do not take tablets at the first sign of illness. All tablets have side effects and the wrong tablet may slow your recovery.

8. Seek medical advice
It is not ideal to be treating yourself. If you have any choice, opt to seek qualified medical advice, especially if you are getting worse. There is no substitute for competent medical advice if you can possibly get it.

SIDE EFFECTS OF MEDICATION

Generally we take a medication or drug because the *benefits* of the drug outweigh the potential *side effects*. Most people do not get major side effects from drugs, but it *is* possible to be the unlucky one. A drug often causes different side effects in different people.

It is possible to confuse the effects of the *disease*, with the effects of the *drug used to treat the disease*. For example: if you feel nauseous while taking an antibiotic, it is hard to tell if you feel that way because you are sick, or because of the medication. Antibiotics generally *do not* make you tired, *being sick* makes you tired.

The most common side effects of drugs are:
Nausea, vomiting, rash, headache, dizziness, diarrhoea.
If the side effect is minor, it is worth persisting with the chosen treatment. If you are in any doubt, or if the side effects seem to be getting worse, stop the treatment and seek medical advice.

The uncommon side effects of drugs are:
Most medications have the potential to cause serious side effects, even death, in an unlucky few. Some people are very sensitive to penicillin and can develop anaphylaxis (severe allergic reaction) which may be fatal if not treated. Some people will get hepatitis from some drugs. These side effects are rare but possible. Of course, take medication only if needed, and seek medical attention as soon as possible if you get worse.

Test dose of an unknown drug before departure
If you have never taken a particular tablet before, take one tablet before you go to test for side effects. The wilds of Africa or Asia are a terrible place to find out you are allergic to a medication.

Consult the reference table
Drug dosages, side effects, cautions, interactions, other names etc are included in the drug reference table at the end of this section (pp 116-123).

Write down here for future reference

Your pulse rate at rest _____ per minute
Adult average is 60-80
Your breathing rate at rest _____per minute
Adult average is 15-20

FEVERS

Normal Body Temperature is 37°C

Why is Fever important?
Fever or 'having a temperature' is a clue that some sort of infection is present. The infection can be due to a virus (e.g. the common cold or flu), a bacteria (e.g. pneumonia, septicemia or typhoid) or other parasites (e.g. malaria, amoeba).

A raised body temperature helps the immune system destroy these agents more quickly. Occasionally fevers can be harmful, especially in very young children.

Sometimes you may feel hot when you do not have a fever. It is important to actually take your temperature, so you can treat yourself most appropriately. For accuracy it is best to take your temperature at least 15 minutes after a hot or cold drink or food. It is useful to write down your temperature and the time it was taken.

Look for an obvious site of infection
Firstly, try and work out what is causing the fever. Do you have any other symptoms? For example sore ears, boils or wounds, a rattly cough producing green phlegm or sputum, diarrhoea with blood in the motions, burning or frequent urination? The fever may be coming from these areas, and if so, these symptoms need to be treated appropriately. Infections which are contained *locally* do not generally cause fever. If you have an infected finger and feel well, the infection is most likely under control, within the confines of your finger. An infected finger *plus* a fever may mean the infection is spreading into your blood stream.

Fever with *no* obvious site of infection may mean the infection is in the bloodstream, e.g. malaria or septicemia. This is very serious.

You should see a doctor immediately if you have..
- Fever with no obvious cause (*Never* assume it is the flu)
- Any fever over 41°C
- Fever associated with headache and neck stiffness
- Any fever which persists more than 48 hours
- A pulse rate that is fast, weakened or irregular
- Difficulty breathing
- Decreased urine output
- Dizziness on standing up or even sitting up

This list is not exhaustive.

Treating a fever
1. Find the source. A fever is best treated by removing the source of the infection. If you are confident the infection is under control, you may treat the *symptom* of fever in order to feel more comfortable.

2. Paracetamol at the usual dose will lower fever.

3. Tepid sponging is an easy way to make a patient feel comfortable. Lukewarm water is sponged onto the body and especially the trunk. Allow the water to evaporate. The process of evaporation will reduce body heat. Do not allow the person to become cold. Shivering will generate more heat.

Fever in a malarious area
Remember no malaria tablet is 100% effective in preventing malaria, so presume *any* fever you develop is due to malaria until proven otherwise. If you get a fever like this, you need to see a doctor within 24 hours. Malaria can be easily treated in the early stages, but if not, it can be fatal.

Not within a week of arriving
A fever developing within one week of arriving in a malarious area, is most *un*likely to be malaria. Malaria has an incubation period of at least a week i.e. at least one week between the mosquito bite and the symptoms developing.

Symptoms of malaria
Malaria usually starts as a flu-like illness. Malaria almost always causes a fever plus any of the following: sweats; shivering; headaches; tiredness; muscle, joint or stomach pains; nausea; vomiting or diarrhoea. You may feel burning hot for a while, and then cold and shivery. This may be followed by sweating and exhaustion or tiredness. Only sometimes is malaria a recurring illness. You may experience fever and chills for a day and then "recover" and feel well. Malaria can imitate other diseases. You *cannot* tell if you have malaria from your symptoms alone. The *only* way to confirm malaria is to have a blood test.

ICT Malaria test kit
If available, a malaria test kit may be used for confirmation of falciparum or cerebral malaria. A finger prick blood sample gives a result in 5 minutes. If the first test is negative and the person remains unwell, the test should be repeated in 24 hours. No reliable test is available for the other strains as yet.

Why use standby treatment of malaria?

Standby treatment is needed when you develop a fever and cannot get medical advice.

The standby treatment for malaria is a temporary measure that will keep the parasites under control while you make your way to medical care.

You can die if your malaria fever is left untreated for as little as *60 hours* (though the average is 4 days). The fever may be due to something simple such as the flu, but it is safer to over-treat the flu in this situation, rather than risk *not treating* malaria.

When to take standby treatment

If medical care is not available within 24 hours, you *should* take the emergency standby treatment, and immediately make your way to good medical care if you develop either of the following:

1. A fever which is present continuously or 'on and off' for more than 48 hours. Malaria is even more likely if you have a fever plus any of the other symptoms previously described.
2. If you have a positive ICT malaria test.

Doses of tablets used for standby treatment:

There are different medications available for standby treatment. Your doctor may prescribe **ONE** of the following for use in emergencies. These are all for adults only.

All tablets should be taken with plenty of water.

1. Lariam = mefloquine 250mg tablets

Important: If you are taking Lariam for prevention, you must not take it for *treatment* unless supervised by a doctor. A severe overdose of Lariam can cause cardiac arrest.

Take Lariam as follows:
i)   take one Maxolon tablet (10mg), wait 30 minutes then
ii) take two Lariam tablets, wait 6 hours then
iii) take one Maxolon tablet (10mg), wait 30 minutes then
iv) if you weigh *60kg or more*: Take 2 further Lariam tabs
                         Total = 4 Lariam tablets.
                or
If you weigh *less than 60kg*: Take 1 further Lariam tab
                         Total = 3 Lariam tablets.

Note: One of the side effects of Lariam is nausea. Feeling feverish will also make you nauseous. This is why you need to take one anti-nausea pill (e.g. Maxolon or Stemetil) 30 minutes before each dose of Lariam.

2. Malarone = atovaquone 25mg + proguanil 100mg

Malarone is a highly effective treatment for malaria in all areas, including very drug resistant areas. No major side effects have been reported from malarone use, however it should be avoided in women who are pregnant or breastfeeding (due to lack of information). A major disadvantage is its cost as it is much more expensive.

Take Malarone with food or a milky drink as follows:
four (4) Malarone tablets at same time each day for 3 days
Total of 12 tablets. A pack contains <u>one</u> course.

3. Fansidar
= sulphadoxine 500mg + pyrimethamine 25mg

Although Fansidar is not recommended for prevention of malaria, it can sometimes be useful for treatment. It is often used for standby treatment in travellers taking Lariam for prevention of malaria. Fansidar should not be taken by those allergic to sulphur drugs.

Take Fansidar as follows: take three tablets all at once.

4. Quinine 300mg tablets

If you are taking Lariam for prevention, you must not take Quinine for treatment unless supervised by a doctor.

Take Quinine as follows:
take two 300mg tablets three times a day for 7 days (total 2 per dose x 3 per day x 7 days = 42 tablets).
Often taken (under medical supervision) with Fansidar or Doxycycline to ensure complete treatment.

5. Halfan = halofantrine 250 mg tablets

Halfan was previously recommended for standby treatment of malaria, however it is no longer recommended due to the likelihood of dangerous side effects - especially heart beat irregularities or 'arrhythmias'. Halfan may still sometimes be used for treatment of malaria under close medical supervision.

6. Cotexin = artemesinin

This medication is not available in Australia but is available in Africa – it contains a form of Artemesinin. This is a fast-acting and effective treatment of malaria, however if used alone, it requires a treatment course of at least SEVEN DAYS or the malaria recurrence rate is 40-50%.

Treatment is often combined with mefloquine (Lariam) to decrease the chance of recurrence.   There is antagonism between Artemesinin and Malarone so they must not be taken together.

7. Chloroquine 150mg base per tablet
(Sometimes chloroquine tablets will say 200mg.   This is usually equivalent to 150mg of *base.*)

To treat malaria, take chloroquine as follows:
i)   day 1 - take four tablets (600mg), wait 6 hours
ii) take two more tablets, then wait until next day
iii) day 2 and day 3 - take two tablets each day
(Total 10 tablets of 150mg)

These are all temporary treatments only
The above treatments do not replace a blood test and proper medical treatment. Standby treatment will however, keep you safe for a few days while you seek help, since delayed or inappropriate treatment of malaria may be fatal. Some strains of malaria hibernate in the liver.

Once you have taken the standby treatment, even if you feel better, you need a blood test and may need further medication to effect a permanent cure.   You may even have another disease and not malaria after all, so it *is* very important to get medical advice as soon as possible.

GUT PROBLEMS IN TRAVELLERS

1. Food poisoning
2. Vomiting
3. Traveller's diarrhoea
4. Constipation

1. Food Poisoning

Food poisoning can happen anywhere, but seems more common in travellers because you 'eat out' such a lot. As one traveller wrote: 'We only ate in restaurants and four star hotels, ..yet I *still* got caught with bad spring rolls.. and was sick for 14 hours. You can never be too careful'.

There are two types of food poisoning. It is important to try and work out which *type* of food poisoning you have, so you know what to do, and how long you are likely to be sick.

Make a guess as to how long it has been between *eating* the suspect food and *getting sick*. The amount of time between eating the 'poisoned' food and getting sick is a good clue to which type of food poisoning you have. (It *can* be hard to distinguish between the two types if you have eaten *numerous* suspect meals.)

Two types of food poisoning

1. Toxin type

This is due to eating food containing bacterial toxins. Germs have been growing in the food before you ate it. As they grew, they released waste products. It is eating these waste products or toxins which makes you sick.

If symptoms develop within 2-12 hours of ingesting the 'poisoned' food, you probably have the 'toxin' type of food poisoning.

The 'toxin' type of food poisoning is usually associated with a lot of vomiting and a little diarrhoea. Your body is trying to get rid of the toxin. Once you have vomited everything out, you get better very quickly. The best treatment for this type of illness is to rest, drink fluids and wait 12-24 hours. Do not take anti-vomiting tablets, as your body needs to get rid of that toxin.

2. Germ type

This type of food poisoning is due to eating food containing a small number of germs, which multiply after they get into your gut and make you sick.

If symptoms develop 12-24 hours or more after ingesting the 'poisoned' food, you probably have the 'germ' type of food poisoning. The 'germ' type of food poisoning takes longer to come on, lasts longer (e.g. several days), and is more likely to cause diarrhoea. 'Germ' type of food poisoning is one of the causes of the famous 'Traveller's Diarrhoea'. (See the following section for how to treat this condition.)

There is some overlap between the two types of food poisoning so you cannot always be certain. Sometimes the 'toxin' type can take up to 24 hours to develop.

2. Vomiting

Vomiting can be due to many things

The most common cause of vomiting in travellers is a toxin or a germ in your gut. However, vomiting may be a sign of more serious illness such as appendicitis.

See a doctor if..

You should see a doctor if you have vomiting *plus*
- fever (remember malaria)
- severe pains in the stomach or anywhere else
- bad headache

- if you are unable to keep down enough fluid to balance what you are losing. (Dehydration can develop rapidly.)
- vomiting continues for more than 24 hours.

Treatment for vomiting

Rest. Drink small amounts of fluid regularly to replace what you are losing. Add Gastrolyte to the fluid to replace lost salts and sugars. Vomiting should settle once your stomach is empty.

Tablets or suppositories to treat the vomiting

If you cannot keep *any* fluids down, you may need to take an antivomiting medication e.g. prochlorperazine (Stemetil) or metoclopramide (Maxolon). These drugs help to break the vicious cycle where dehydration makes you feel terrible so you are unable to keep down fluids, leading to more dehydration.

One of the problems with vomiting is you may not keep tablets down. Stemetil suppositories may be useful under these circumstances, or you may need an injection. Do not take anti-nausea medications for more than 24 hours without medical advice.

3. Travellers diarrhoea

Traveller's diarrhoea means *loose* or *more frequent* bowel motions while travelling.

If you normally have one motion per day, then three motions per day is considered traveller's diarrhoea. Much of the time, this apparent misbehaviour of the bowels does not affect your travel plans. It is more interesting than intrusive.

Diarrhoea affects up to 50% of travellers visiting developing countries. There are many different causes for diarrhoea, but usually traveller's diarrhoea is caused by an unfamiliar germ infecting the bowel. The germ may be perfectly harmless to the local inhabitants. Occasionally, diarrhoea may be a symptom of bowel irritation from unusual or spicy foods or may even be due to other diseases such as malaria, or typhoid.

Many first time travellers find that bowels and particularly 'poo' are strange subjects for conversation. To make it sound better, travellers diarrhoea is often given exotic local names; e.g. Bali belly, Delhi belly, Montezuema's revenge or Pharaoh's curse. Guide books talk about bowel motions, bowel actions, faeces, or stools. It's all poo, and too much is not a good thing.

If diarrhoea is merely interesting and you feel well in yourself, it is best to leave your bowels to sort it out for themselves.

Unfortunately it is not always so easy.

As well as your bowels wanting to empty more often, they may bloat, gurgle and cramp up, causing considerable pain. They may demand to be emptied immediately and even cause you to have an 'accident' on the way to the toilet. Wind passed from the bowels may smell quite dreadful, and you may experience burning, stinging or pain in your bottom during or after a bowel action: the so-called 'ring of fire'. Your stomach may be affected and make you feel nauseous and you may even vomit. Your whole system may be thrown out of kilter and you may get a temperature (over 37°C) and feel generally terrible, tired, weak or washed out.

Traveller's diarrhoea generally lasts 1 to 5 days and usually goes away without treatment. Proximity to a toilet and adequate supplies of toilet paper are helpful. However, the following suggestions will minimise the discomfort.

What to do when you have Traveller's diarrhoea...

Remember, diarrhoea is contagious.
Don't give it to your friends. You should wash your hands meticulously after going to the toilet and before eating. Do not share towels or toothbrushes. Avoid sharing water bottles or plates, spoons etc while you have the diarrhoea.

For the first 24 hours:
If the diarrhoeal illness is mild, the best thing for the first 24 hours is to avoid pills, rest, and follow the eating and drinking guidelines below. If it is the toxin type of food poisoning, your symptoms will go away without treatment.

What to drink when you have diarrhoea
The best liquid to drink during an attack of diarrhoea is rehydration solution (Gastrolyte blackcurrant flavour).
Drink one dose after each loose motion. The dose should be made up accurately so it will have the maximum effect. Add one sachet or two tablets of Gastrolyte to 200mls of water. Rehydration solution is an effective, drug-free method of speeding your recovery. The secret to keeping fluid down is to drink small amounts frequently.

If packaged solutions are not available you can make up your own rehydration solution by *adding 8 level teaspoons of sugar, and half a teaspoon of salt to one litre of water.*

You can also supplement your fluid intake with mineral water, weak tea, fruit juice or water. Ensure the water is not contaminated. Aim to drink *at least* four litres of liquid per day. In some diarrhoeal diseases you may lose eight litres of fluid from the bowels each day, so you would need to drink at least eight to ten litres. Drink enough liquid to replace what is being lost, and you will be fine. Most important with diarrhoea - no booze!

What to eat when you have diarrhoea

You do need to eat. Do not starve yourself. In the past experts recommended no food for 24 hours to 'rest the bowel'. Further research has found this is *not* the best thing to do. It seems the 'good' bacteria which normally live in the bowel, actually assist in the absorption of water. These bacteria need starch in order to absorb the water efficiently. Rehydration powders have been developed which include rice starch, but they taste pretty dreadful.

It is now recommended you drink fluids *and eat starch.* Any type of starch will do e.g. cooked rice or rice cereal, cooked oats or porridge, wheat (toast), or mashed potato. A small amount of extra salt can be added. Ripe bananas are also recommended, as they are a good source of potassium.

Minimise the use of dairy products until your motions look normal. You should avoid spicy foods while you have diarrhoea.

The consistency of your motions is a useful guide to the consistency of food you should eat. If your bowel motions are watery, your diet should be very watery e.g runny porridge. As your motions become more formed or solid, you can eat food that is more solid.

Three things to check when you have diarrhoea

In order to treat diarrhoea most effectively, you must do three things:

1. Take your temperature

Normal body temperature is 37°C.

2. Look at the bowel motions

Check for consistency (watery, semi-formed or normal). It is important to note if any blood or mucous is present.

3. Watch your fluid balance

Fluid balance is the difference between what goes *in* (what you eat and drink) and what comes *out* (of your bladder and bowels). Make a rough guess about whether you are *losing* more fluid than you are *drinking*.

If your fluid intake is sufficient, your urine will be a pale yellow colour. The sensation of thirst is not a reliable indicator. If you feel thirsty, you are at least mildly dehydrated.

When you must see a doctor
- If your temperature is over 40°C.
- If your bowel motions contain blood.
- If you experience sudden onset of profuse, very watery diarrhoea; dehydration can develop within a few hours.
- If you are unable to drink enough fluid to compensate for what is lost through diarrhoea.
- If the diarrhoea lasts longer than two weeks.

Two types of tablets for diarrhoea
There are two types of pills for diarrhoea: Stoppers and Antibiotics.

1. Stoppers paralyse the bowel and *ease the symptoms.* e.g. loperamide (Imodium), Lomotil, Buscopan
2. Antibiotics *kill germs* and treat the cause e.g., norfloxacin (Noroxin), cotrimoxazole (Bactrim), tinidazole (Fasigyn).

When you get 'the diarrhoea' you can choose to either wait it out or take tablets. As previously noted, most traveller's diarrhoea will go away without treatment in one to five days. In the past, most experts recommended waiting, resting and drinking fluids.

Research now suggests that in many cases, you will decrease your illness from several days to one day by taking an anti-diarrhoeal stopper plus an antibiotic.

Many travellers are keen to cure themselves as fast as possible, so they do not lose valuable travelling time. The following guidelines plus the flow chart on page 91 will help you use the tablets correctly.

Take the stoppers if diarrhoea is inconvenient

Diarrhoea is caused by a germ infecting the bowel.
Taking a stopper is not really a treatment, and does not kill germs. Instead of being flushed out by the diarrhoea, the germs are held 'inside' and may have a lovely time attacking the wall of your bowel. Stoppers can be used safely if you follow the guidelines.

Stoppers are especially useful when travelling e.g. if diarrhoea is a serious inconvenience whilst travelling on a raft, or even on a bus. Antibiotics can be used with stoppers.

If diarrhoea is inconvenient, your temperature is normal (37°C), and there is *no* blood or mucous in the motions, you may take a 'stopper' e.g. loperamide (Imodium). Lomotil is another common 'stopper'. Loperamide (Imodium) usually has fewer side effects than Lomotil. Lomotil may cause dry mouth, drowsiness, and blurred vision. Stoppers such as loperamide (Imodium) work by paralysing the bowel.

Loperamide (Imodium): Take two capsules at once, followed by one capsule after each loose motion to a maximum of eight capsules per day. Do not take them for more than 48 hours at a time.

Buscopan: Sometimes traveller's diarrhoea is associated with quite painful stomach cramps and you may need a more specific antispasmodic e.g. hyoscine butylbromide (Buscopan). The dose is 20mg (= 2x10mg tablets) four times daily. If pain persists then see a doctor.

Four situations where you may need an antibiotic

1. If you have more than 4 motions in 24 hours
Profuse diarrhoea suggests a serious germ. If you have four or more loose bowel motions in 24 hours you may consider taking an antibiotic. If you have more than 6 loose motions, definitely take the antibiotic. If you do *not* have a fever, and the diarrhoea is also very inconvenient you may take a stopper e.g. loperamide *as well*.

2. If you have diarrhoea + temperature over 39°C
Fever plus diarrhoea suggests a more serious germ. Take *only* the antibiotic. *Do not take loperamide* as it will keep the germs in contact with the bowel wall for longer, and cause further damage. Diarrhoea is nature's way of 'flushing out' a bowel infection.

3. If there is blood or mucous in the bowel motion
Blood, in particular, in your motions suggests the bowel wall has been penetrated. This is usually due to a more serious germ. Take *only* the antibiotic. *Do not take the stopper, loperamide.*

Regardless of what happens, if you have had blood in the motions, you should see a doctor when you can, so you can have a test and ensure the germs are gone.

4. If you still have diarrhoea after a few days
If you are experiencing up to three motions per day and it has gone on for more than 48 hours, despite fluids and possibly stoppers, try the antibiotic.

How to take antibiotics for diarrhoea
Without a microscopic examination of the bowel motion, we cannot be sure which germ is causing the diarrhoea, so a calculated guess is required. Currently the 'best guess' antibiotic is:

Norfloxacin (Noroxin) 400mg: The usual recommended dose is 400mg (1 tablet) twice a day for 3 days = 6 tablets total. However it will work faster if you take the first two tablets together - to really knock the germs hard to start - and then follow up with one tablet every 12 hours for the subsequent doses. Take the tablets one hour before or two hours after food. Iron or multivitamin preparations containing zinc should be avoided while taking norfloxacin, as they decrease absorption of the drug from the stomach.

Alternatives for self treatment of diarrhoea are:
Cotrimoxazole 160/800 (Bactrim DS, Septrin forte): 1 tablet twice a day for 3 days.
Ciprofloxacin (Ciproxin) 500mg: 2 tablets at once.

If there is no improvement after the antibiotic
See a doctor if you are not much better within 24 hours of taking the antibiotic, particularly if you have a fever or temperature. Be suspicious when treating any fever with antibiotics. Sometimes other diseases manifest as diarrhoea and fever - it may be Malaria. If you cannot see a doctor and you have persistent diarrhoea, there are two other common things which it may be: Amoebic Dysentery or Giardia. The following guidelines may be helpful.

Continued blood in the motions
Amoebic dysentery often causes blood or mucous in the motions. Other symptoms may include fever, abdominal pain and weight loss. These symptoms may be hard to distinguish from bacterial diarrhoea. If you have taken norfloxacin for bloody diarrhoea with no improvement after 48 hours and you cannot find a doctor, it is worth trying a 3 day course of tinidazole in case it is Amoebic Dysentery.

Tinidazole (Fasigyn, Simplotan) 500mg per tablet. Take 4 tablets daily for 3 days. You must avoid alcohol for 48 hours after each dose or you will experience a terrible hangover.

If the diarrhoea lasts for longer than 7 days
There are many causes of persistent diarrhoea. If you have not already done so, try a course of Noroxin (antibiotic). Giardia is probably the most common cause of persistent diarrhoea among travellers. It is especially common among backpackers in developing countries e.g. India and Nepal.

Flow Chart for Treatment of Diarrhoea in Adults

Loose or watery bowel motions, Nausea and/or Vomiting. Abdominal cramps especially before bowel action.

'*Rx*' = 'Treatment'.
This flow chart is a guide only and does not replace consultation with a competent doctor.
Never forget: If you have visited a malarious area, any fever could be malaria until proven otherwise.

Rx For first 24 hours rest, avoid alcohol, increase intake of clear fluids. Take GASTROLYTE. Aim for one dose after each loose motion. Eat some starch e.g. cooked rice, potatoes, wheat. The consistency of your diet should roughly parallel the consistency of the motions. Take your temperature. If the illness is mild, wait at least 24 hours before taking any medication.

Passage of the 4th loose, watery motion in 24 hours? —— Yes → **48 hours after taking antibiotic..... Has there been a big improvement?**

No ↓

Temperature over 38.5°C? —— Yes →

No ↓

Is there blood in the motions? —— Yes →

No ↓

Is diarrhoea very inconvenient? —— Yes →
Are toilets unavailable?

No ↓

Rx (Stopper)
LOPERAMIDE
2 caps to start and then 1 after every loose motion, max 8 per day.
Do not take for longer than 1 day.
—— Yes ↑

Rx (Antibiotic)
NORFLOXACIN
Take 2 x 400mg tablets to start and then one every 12 hours. Total 6 tablets.

Avoid antacids, Iron and multivitamin preparations containing Zinc while taking Norfloxacin.

Not improving? Still unwell 48 hours after onset of first symptom? →

Rx
Continue fluids and rest. Most travellers diarrhoea will settle within 5 days.

Has the diarrhoea lasted more than 1 week? Do you also have excess gas; burping, bloating, flatus)? (Some describe it as rotten egg)? Giardia →

Rx (Antibiotic)
TINIDAZOLE
4 x 500mg tabs all at once. No alcohol for 48 hrs.

48 hours after taking antibiotic..... Has there been a big improvement?

No → Is there blood in the motions?
Yes → ?Amoebic Dysentery →
Rx (Antibiotic)
TINIDAZOLE
4 x 500mg tabs daily for 3 days.

No → Finish course of antibiotics.

Yes... Good finish antibiotic → Do you have a fever?
No → Finish course of antibiotics.
Yes →

No improvement by 24 hrs after finishing the course? →

See a Doctor immediately

Other germs can also cause persistent diarrhoea. Determining the exact germ requires a microscopic examination of the offending motion. If you have tried norfloxacin, treat persistent diarrhoea as Giardia and see a doctor when possible if symptoms persist.

Classic symptoms of Giardia

The diarrhoea is characteristically *mild*, just a few extra motions a day for several weeks. The persistence of diarrhoea is a key clue to the presence of Giardia. The motions are usually loose but not liquid. They may smell very bad. Giardia does not cause blood in the motions or fever. Your motions may be painful to pass, or you may have stomach cramps just prior to passing a motion. You may pass offensive smelling wind from your bottom, feel bloated in the stomach, and burp more than usual. Burps which taste of 'rotten eggs' are characteristic. Some people lose their appetite, and may lose some weight. Under the microscope, the Giardia germ looks like the drawing below.

Antibiotics for Giardia

Giardia does not respond to regular antibiotics. Treat as follows:

Tinidazole 500mg per tablet (Simplotan or Fasigyn) ; Take 4 tablets all at once for one day only. It is a long acting preparation and stays in your system for several days after the four tablets.

No alcohol should be taken for 48 hours after these tablets or you will experience an exaggerated hangover.

Metronidazole 400mg tabs (Flagyl) is another tablet commonly used for this condition. Metronidazole is not as popular amongst travellers since it requires a much longer course - one 400mg tablet must be taken three times a day for seven days.

Cyclospora

Cyclospora is a recently discovered germ that causes persistent diarrhoea in travellers. It typically causes profuse diarrhoea, abdominal pain, nausea, tiredness and lack of appetite.

If you have tried norfloxacin and tinidazole with no improvement and cannot get to a doctor, try the following;
Cotrimoxazole 160/800 (Bactrim DS, Septrin Forte)
Take 1 tablet twice daily for 10 days.

4. Constipation

Contrary to what most people expect, many travellers get constipated. Constipation is usually due to prolonged sitting while travelling, change of diet and even too many diarrhoea pills. Lack of safe drinking water may also lead to dehydration and worsen the constipation.

Simple treatments

The best treatment for constipation is to drink more fluids, eat more fibre and get more exercise. A fibre supplement (e.g. Fybogel, Metamucil) may help 'get things moving'.

Medication

If the constipation is more severe and you are feeling uncomfortable, a mild laxative (e.g. Coloxyl) is useful. It is normally taken before bed for two to three nights. Do not be tempted to overdose or you may get diarrhoea and cramping stomach pains.

COUGHS, COLDS, CHEST INFECTIONS

Problems of the lungs, sinuses, nose and throat affect up to 20% of travellers. Symptoms may be due to either an allergy or an infection. The infection can be caused by either a virus or a bacteria. A runny nose with sneezing and itchy eyes suggests an allergy. A runny, blocked nose with a sore throat, suggests a cold. Cough, sore throat and aches and pains in the muscles suggests the flu. 'Colds' and 'flu' are both *viral* conditions. A cough producing green phlegm suggests bronchitis or *bacterial* infection.

General treatment

Many preparations are available to minimise the symptoms. General measures are important: rest, increase fluids, and take paracetamol, or cough and cold medicines (Orthoxicol, Sudafed etc) as necessary. Vitamins C and B are advocated by some authorities. Stop smoking. Take your temperature.

When you must see a doctor...

Most cases of flu or respiratory infection will go away without treatment. However, you need to see a doctor if any of the following develop.

- If your temperature is over 40°C
- If you cough up large amounts of green mucous or blood
- Fever with extremely sore throat
- If symptoms persist for more than one week.

Allergies

Sneezing, itchy eyes, and runny nose suggest an allergy, also known as hay fever. Most allergy sufferers will be familiar with the symptoms. Allergies are rather common among travellers. There are many new things to be allergic to. Developing countries may have a lot of dust, or smog. Try to minimise contact with the cause of your allergy. It may be necessary to place a scarf over your nose and mouth when travelling in dusty environments. Treatment includes antihistamine medications e.g. Teldane, Hismanal, Avil or Phenergan. Nasal sprays, especially steroid based nasal sprays, e.g. Aldecin or Beconase are also quite effective. Take two puffs in each nostril, twice a day.

If you have the flu

The flu is a distinct illness. Symptoms of the flu are high fever, cough, aches and pains in muscles and tiredness.

The flu is caused by a virus and antibiotics will not help.

When to take antibiotics for a chest infection

You probably need antibiotics if you have a temperature >39.5°C plus a moist or rattly cough, and you are coughing up green or blood-tinged sputum.

Early treatment with antibiotics (e.g. roxithromycin, amoxycillin or doxycycline) will stop this condition getting worse. See a doctor if possible. Bacterial chest infections are especially common in smokers.

Persistent dry cough

After a viral illness or flu, it is common to develop a persistent dry cough. The best treatment is to drink fluids and take a cough suppressant at night if the cough disturbs your sleep. If the cough persists more than 3 weeks you should see a doctor.

SKIN DAMAGE

The skin is the 'defence' line between the environment and ourselves so it does take a bit of damage from time to time. Travellers' skin damage is discussed in the following sections;

- bleeding - wounds and nose bleeds
- wound care including cuts, grazes, burns
- bites including insects and bigger animals
- rashes

Bleeding

Bleeding wounds

If helping others wear disposable gloves, if possible, to minimise contact with blood. For at least 3 minutes, apply firm pressure to the bleeding wound with a large dressing or clean handkerchief. Do not use a tourniquet. If there is a foreign object in the wound, apply pressure around the wound or on the heart side of the wound. Never remove large foreign objects embedded in a wound or the bleeding may get much worse. Keep the pressure on, until the bleeding stops. If possible, raise the bleeding part above the level of the heart. If a lot of blood is lost, keep the injured person warm by wrapping them in an emergency blanket, and keep them lying down. Seek medical attention urgently.

Nose bleeds

Sit up and hold the nostrils closed by pinching the soft fleshy parts together. If available, place a cold pack on the bridge of the nose. Be patient. In most cases the bleeding will stop within 15 minutes. If not, see a doctor.

Wound care checklist

Step 1. Adequate cleaning

The presence of *some* bacteria in the wound is to be expected. Bacteria are everywhere in the environment. Problems occur when there are too *many* bacteria growing in the wound. Infection will delay healing. In the tropics, minor cuts and scratches will rapidly become infected if not treated correctly. Once established, tropical ulcers may be hard to cure. Do not ignore minor wounds as you might at home. Infection can be prevented by the following:

1. Always wash your hands with soap and water before handling wounds. Try to touch the wound as little as possible. Ensure all dressings are sterile.

2. Clean all wounds thoroughly at the outset. Inspect all wounds under a good light to check for foreign particles - these must be removed. Dirt, gravel, marine slime or other foreign particles will cause infection. Adequate cleaning is especially important for deep wounds or contaminated wounds. Irrigate wounds with *room temperature* sterile (boiled or bottled) water or salt solution. *Add one quarter teaspoon of salt to 200 mls (1 cup) of clean water.* Pour water over the wound or use a 5 or 10ml syringe to squirt water gently onto the wound to remove foreign matter. Note that marine slime may not be visible. Pour diluted

hydrogen peroxide on the wound if available. The foaming action helps dislodge foreign particles. Wounds potentially contaminated by coral need to be gently scrubbed with a clean toothbrush or piece of gauze to remove particles of marine slime, even if they look quite clean.

3. Dead tissue must be removed as it blocks healing and acts as a breeding ground for germs. Cut away obvious bits of dead tissue with sharp scissors. This is known as 'debridement'.

Step 2. Use of antiseptic
After cleaning the wound, apply a thin layer of iodine based antiseptic e.g. betadine. *If you have an allergy to iodine, use only the salt solution for wound cleansing.*

Step 3. Ensure the wound edges are touching
The body quickly forms a bridge between two pieces of living tissue if they are touching: i.e. neatly lined up and held together. Gaping wounds heal more slowly, so suturing, applying steristrips, or just a firm dressing should be used to bring the wound edges together and keep them properly aligned.

Note that small cuts on the fingers are usually not sutured, as the blood supply is so good, that these wounds heal quite fast anyway. Wounds on the scalp can sometimes be held together by tying two pieces of hair together across the wound.

When pulling deep wounds together, you need to make sure you do not just pull the top layers of the wound together leaving a hole or space beneath. If the surface of the wound heals first, a space may be left underneath where debris can collect (see diagram).

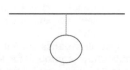

Debris accumulates in this space and cannot get out. This delays healing.

Where wound edges cannot be easily brought together (e.g. gaping wounds, burns, ulcers) the wound needs to heal from the base up. It may sometimes be necessary to pack a wound with gauze to prevent this space forming. Packing the wound involves gently placing tightly packed, moist, sterile gauze into the wound to keep the top of the wound open until the base heals. Make sure a tail of gauze is left coming out of the wound so the gauze can be easily removed when the wound is re-dressed.

Step 4. Choose the best dressing

All wounds should be covered for protection, so the wound will not become contaminated after the injury. It is especially important with larger wounds to avoid the wound coming into contact with sea water which may be potentially contaminated, so unless the dressing is waterproof, it is best to avoid swimming until the wound is healed.

The 'right' dressing depends on whether the wound is closed or open.

Closed wounds

In closed wounds, the edges of the wound are brought together (e.g. sutured), and most of the damaged area is hidden away below the normal skin. These wounds heal fastest if kept dry, especially for the first 48 to 72 hours. For these wounds, choose a dry, non-adherent dressing such as Melolin, Primopore or even a bandaid. Dressings may initially need to be changed daily, as a little ooze may occur through the suture line in the first few days.

Open wounds

In open wounds, the damaged tissue is in contact with the outside environment such as ulcers, grazes, burns etc. All the evidence from current research shows these types of wounds get less infection, **feel better and heal faster** (in some studies up to four days faster) **if kept moist.**

The natural ooze from wounds contains:
i) white blood cells which protect the wound from infection
ii) enzymes to break down dead tissues
iii) numerous vital growth factors which coordinate wound healing
iv) nutrients which feed the growing tissues
v) water itself, which is necessary for normal metabolism of cells, protects nerve endings from drying out, and stops the healing wound sticking to the dressing and thus being damaged when the dressing is removed.

'Moist' or 'occlusive' dressings (e.g. Opsite) are recommended for open wounds. These dressings are made from a special type of plastic, designed to hold this 'ooze' in place.

Sometimes there is a great deal of 'ooze', and an absorbent material (e.g. IntraSite or SoloSite gel) is needed under the dressing to hold the 'ooze', while still keeping the wound surface moist.

For small open wounds, keeping the wound moist is less critical, and elastoplast plastic strips or bandaids are adequate.

For larger open wounds, after wound cleaning, ensure the area around the wound is dry and seal with an Opsite dressing or similar product. You may need to shave the surrounding area to ensure the dressing will stick. Ideally leave the dressing untouched for 3-7 days. Sometimes the edges lift and the dressing falls off, so it does not last the full 7 days. If the dressing falls off or needs to be removed, reapply by repeating steps one to four above. Note that Opsite dressing is waterproof if applied correctly. In difficult areas (elbows, knees) a dry, non stick dressing with a bandage may be easier to apply than a waterproof, moist wound dressing like Opsite.

Step 5. Monitor the wound

You will automatically monitor the wound by noticing each day whether the wound feels better or worse. This is one of the best guides to successful healing. If a wound is healing properly it will feel better each day.

Some dressings are 'see through' so you can look at the wound without removing the dressing. At the very least, you must inspect the wound under a good light with each dressing change. Sometimes it may help to measure the *depth* and *width* of the wound, so you can check the progress objectively. Also note the colour of the wound. New growth (granulation tissue) is usually quite red and looks clean. Very white tissue is usually dead, painless to touch and should be removed.

Different dressings need to be changed at different intervals:
Moist dressings e.g. Opsite - every 3 to 7 days
Dry, non stick dressings e.g. Melolin - daily

Note that the most suitable dressing for the wound may change over time.

How fast should wounds heal? The rate of wound healing varies enormously from wound to wound, and person to person. The healing rate depends on many factors such as:
- age and general health of the casualty,
- where the wound is located,
- how the wound occurred (clean cut or crushed tissue),
- how the wound is treated.

Most wounds should be healed in one to two weeks, however it may take many months for the scar to reach full strength.

That is why many scars widen over time, especially if wounds are on sites such as the knee where they are continually stretched.

Watch every wound closely for the following signs of significant infection:

- increasing pain - this is a very important signal that the wound is not healing properly,
- increasing redness, especially if it is spreading in a line away from the wound,
- increasing discharge, especially if discharge is yellow, green, grey or smelly,
- wound bleeding easily when touched,
- fever and increasing pulse rate.

Step 6. Treat infection quickly

If infection sets in *despite* good wound management, the damage can be minimised if the infection is treated early.
If any of the above symptoms develop:

1. check again there is no foreign matter or dead tissue in the wound. If so, it must be removed.
2. you need to seek medical advice and will probably require antibiotics.

The following antibiotics may be appropriate. (Consult the drug reference table for full details of doses etc for these medications)

Cephalexin 500mg Take two tablets to start, and then one every 12 hours for 5 days.
Alternatives; flucloxacillin, roxithromycin, doxycycline

Burns

Burns are a special type of wound. Unlike cuts, or grazes, tissue damage continues to occur for a time after the acute injury due to the presence of heat in the wound.

Cool the area

Do not delay treatment by attempting to remove burned clothing, however you need to remove rings or watches immediately.

The injured area needs immediate cooling with clean, cool water. If you remove the heat, there will be less damage to the tissue. If used, cold packs should be wrapped in a cloth, so you do not freeze skin which is already damaged.

If the skin is blistered and not broken, resist the temptation to burst any blisters that form. The blister provides a clean cover for the damaged area. Beneath the blister, the wound is bathed in a beneficial fluid. If the blister fluid turns cloudy, then it should be burst and the dead skin gently removed.

The wound should be managed as outlined previously, i.e. cleaned with a salt solution, a thin layer of antiseptic applied, and covered with a 'moist dressing' e.g. Opsite.

See a doctor if..
- the burn involves the face or hands,
- the burn is larger in size than the casualty's palm,
- the burned area is not painful - suggesting a full thickness burn,
- signs of infection develop e.g. if the redness extends, the burn becomes more painful or if you develop a fever - a course of antibiotics may be required.

Sunburn
Sunburn can be extremely painful. You may require pain killers. If blistering occurs, the treatment is the same as described above for other burns. Moisturisers are soothing on unbroken skin if they have been stored in the fridge.

Dehydration may occur along with the sunburn. Avoid further sun exposure. Have yearly checkups for skin cancers.

Bites

Insect bites
Bites from fleas, sandflies, mosquitoes, bees, wasps, ticks or leeches are annoying and may even transmit disease.

Care of all insect bites
The odd insect bite needs no particular treatment. If you receive many bites or the insect leaves a small wound, then these bite wounds should be managed as per the wound checklist previously described i.e. wash the site of the bite and apply antiseptic.

Provided the bite is not infected, steroid creams can be applied twice a day for the first 24 hours to decrease the itch and irritation. Stingose gel will also ease the itch.

Holding an ice cube on the itchy spot will give instant relief.

Removing a tick

If a tick is found attached: press down around the tick's head with tweezers, grab the head, and gently pull upwards. Avoid pulling the rear of the body, since this ruptures the tick's internal gut, squeezing the contents out through the attached mouthparts into the victim. Smearing chemicals on the tick will not make it 'let go', and is not recommended. If a tick bite becomes infected, or you notice a rash or funny lump at the bite site, see a doctor. Ticks may carry disease and you may require antibiotics e.g. doxycycline.

Scorpions

These are common in Africa, Central & South America, the Caribbean and less frequently in Asia. Scorpions are active at night. During the day they hide under rocks or in shoes. They bite only when molested. The sting is very painful but does not poison the body. The pain can be alleviated by an injection of local anaesthetic, so if possible see a doctor.

Snakes

Treat all snake bites as poisonous, but it may be comforting to know that most bites are not poisonous. Identify the snake *from a distance* (or there may be more snake bites to treat). Take written notes of the size, colouring, and unusual markings. In Australia - do not wipe the bite site as spilled venom around the wound can help identify the snake. In other countries you may wash the bite site. Bandage the whole of the bitten limb firmly starting from the trunk and working towards the fingers or toes. Do not use the affected limb - add a splint to immobilise the affected limb – this immobilisation stops the poison spreading. Do not 'suck out the poison'. Send someone for help and get medical attention ASAP.

Dog / monkey / cat / bat bites

There are two main concerns after an animal bite:
1. Infection *Wash and dress the wound.* Any animal bite or scratch should be washed with copious amounts of soap and water for 5-10 minutes. Water should be poured onto the wound. Do not scrub the bite site as this can push the infection deeper. It should then be treated as per wound checklist. Antiseptic should be applied and the dressing changed appropriately.
2. Rabies. *See a doctor immediately.* If you are in a rabies infected country you will need post-bite Rabies vaccine. Do not delay. *Any* animal in a rabies area should be suspected of having rabies. Even a vaccinated animal can carry rabies. Vaccination *of animals* is not 100% effective; a study in Thailand showed 3-6% of rabid dogs had been vaccinated.

Never delay vaccination while the animal is observed for signs of rabies.

The safest rabies vaccine is the human diploid cell vaccine. Animal based vaccines are cheaper, but have more side effects. Modern rabies vaccines are not given into the stomach(!?!). Ensure all injections are given with sterile needles and syringes. Chloroquine, alcohol and immunosuppressive drugs should be avoided during the course of rabies vaccine as they interfere with the vaccine. A common post-bite regime is as follows: (Day 0 should be the day of the bite, but it is *never* too late to start.)

i) If you *have* been previously vaccinated, two doses of vaccine are given in the upper arm, one each on day 0, 3.

ii) If you *have not* been previously vaccinated, 5 doses of vaccine are given in the upper arm, one each on day 0, 3, 7, 14, and 28. The goal is for the vaccine to induce protective immunity before the virus gets established. On day 0, you also need rabies immunoglobulin (RI). The dose is 20 IU (International Units) per kg of body weight. This is injected into the wound to neutralise the virus locally and provide protective antibodies while the vaccine takes effect.

If you do get bitten, make sure you seek advice from a reputable source. There have been reports of bite victims being injected with fraudulent vaccines or plain water. Misinformation can also be fatal.

A while ago, an American priest in Bangladesh was bitten by a dog. The local doctor told him 'Don't worry, we have no rabies in this district, you do not need vaccination'. Three weeks later the priest was evacuated to Bangkok with symptoms of rabies encephalitis. He was fully conscious almost to the end and kept a tape recorded diary of his symptoms, signs and feelings while he was dying.

Marine bites and stings

It is best to seek local advice. Treatment varies depending on the cause as there are many dangerous marine creatures: sea wasps, jellyfish, bluebottle, stonefish, fire coral etc. (Australia has some of the worst.) Generally, jellyfish tentacles should be inactivated by pouring vinegar over them. Remove adherent tentacles by scraping with a knife or piece of wood. Rubbing the wound with bare hands or wet sand should be avoided as it causes further discharge of the stinging cells. Stingose gel, local anaesthetic ointment, calamine lotion, or cold packs should be applied. If the pain is severe, you need to seek urgent medical advice. Monitor the casualty in case breathing or circulation is affected.

Skin Rashes

The first question to ask yourself if you get a rash is -

Has there been recent exposure to irritants?

Chemicals, plants or insect bites may cause an allergic rash, sometimes called allergic dermatitis. Have you been swimming in schistomiasis areas? Try an antihistamine or mild steroid cream (e.g. Cortaid) twice a day. Placing an ice cube over the itchy spot will give immediate relief from the itch. Avoid further contact with the offending agent.

Here are descriptions of some common skin rashes in travellers:

Ring shaped rash with flaking edges?

This may be due to a fungus, known as Ringworm (because of the shape - there is no actual worm.) Anti-fungal cream (e.g. clotrimazole, Canesten) should be rubbed on the outer (growing) edges of the ring three times a day. This rash may take three weeks to clear. Ringworms are very contagious. Wash you hands thoroughly after touching it.

Skin between your toes affected?

Flaking, soggy skin between the toes is characteristic of tinea or 'athletes foot'. It is another fungal infection. The fungus thrives in moist conditions. Try to keep the area dry. Use anti-fungal cream twice a day. If possible, put antifungal powder (e.g. tolnaftate) in your socks.

Itchy rash in the armpit, waist or between thighs?

These symptoms usually occur when travelling in a hot climate. They may be due to one of two things:

1. Prickly Heat. You can usually see small blisters in the area of the rash. Prickly heat occurs in very hot climates when profuse sweating leads to blockage of the sweat glands. You need to keep the area as cool and dry as possible. Wear loose, pale coloured, *cotton* clothes. Nylon clothing will aggravate the problem. Use soap sparingly. Soap may further block the sweat glands. Keep your whole body cool to minimise sweating. Apply a warm towel over the area. Salicylic acid solution (Isophyl) should be applied to the rash three times a day.

2. Fungal rashes may also occur in these areas. Fungal rashes look like small red spots which may join together. The best treatment is to keep the area dry and cool (as above for prickly heat) and apply an antifungal cream.

HANGOVERS

This section has been added at the request of several travellers who wrote "Of course it's better to avoid such things, but it's easy to get carried away when one is on holidays. Is there anything that can be done for a hangover?"

Avoidance is certainly the most effective way of dealing with hangovers, but in the real world, there are a few useful facts to know.

The most important thing you can do is to drink plenty of water. The major symptoms of a hangover are caused by dehydration. Drink as much water as possible before you go to bed. Alcohol often causes interrupted sleep, so place a jug of water beside your bed and if you wake up, drink some water during the night.

Alcohol also decreases your blood sugar level. Food or a sweet drink can sometimes make you feel better. If you feel very nauseous, it is better to vomit and empty your stomach. Once your stomach is empty, Maxolon or Stemetil tablets are useful if the nausea persists. Rest will help. Do not drive while you have a hangover. Your blood alcohol level may still be above the legal limit.

The list of alleged cures for a hangover is very long. Unfortunately, nothing, including strong coffee, will make you metabolise the alcohol faster. Berocca is popular to replace B vitamins lost through drinking. It also provides a little sugar.

HOT CLIMATE PROBLEMS

Dehydration and Heat Stroke

Dehydration and heat stroke may be hard to recognise. People remain mildly dehydrated for hours or days, when a slightly increased fluid intake would make them feel much better.

Symptoms of heat stress

Mild dehydration causes tiredness and headache. As you become more dehydrated, you will feel thirsty.

As the condition progresses, further symptoms which may develop are dizziness, nausea, and profuse sweating. This stage is called 'heat exhaustion' because of the extreme tiredness.

Heat exhaustion can rapidly turn into heat stroke which is much more serious. The key question to ask is "Is the patient sweating?" The clue to the presence of heat stroke is that *sweating stops* and the body temperature rises. Unusual behaviour may occur. Watch for this in your companions. Judgement is impaired with heat problems. The affected person may be the last to realise their predicament.

Treatment of Heat Stroke

Cooling is the most important treatment. Drink cool fluids in copious quantities (1-2 litres). Get out of the sun and heat. Find shade or air conditioning and lie down. Avoid activity. Activity generates heat in the muscles which makes the problem worse. Have a cool bath. Do not bathe in really cold water, as this will shut down circulation to your skin and keep the heat in. For severe symptoms you should see a doctor as soon as possible.

COLD CLIMATE PROBLEMS

Frostbite

Frostbite occurs when the skin and blood vessels become extremely cold and freeze. Ice forms inside the cells and the tiny capillaries are destroyed. The condition is most common in the extremities e.g. nose, ears, toes, and fingers.

Cold skin initially just feels cold. The next step is tingling in the extremity. If your fingers or toes start to tingle they need to be warmed immediately. If the area stops hurting, the problem may not have gone away – it may mean the situation is getting worse. Do not attempt to warm the area unless you will remain in that warm environment. Tissue that is partly warmed and freezes again is more susceptible to gangrene. The best way to warm cold extremities is to place them against warm bare skin.

Frostbite is characterised by numbness of the area and whiteness of the affected skin - this is serious and needs medical attention. It is difficult to predict how much long term damage there will be just by looking at the damaged tissues. Ibuprofen has been shown in some trials to improve the survival of cells at the edge of the frost bitten area.

Hypothermia

Hypothermia means low body temperature. The body has become so cold that it cannot function.

The symptoms are confusion, fatigue, and a change of personality.

Mild hypothermia is best treated by seeking warm shelter and drinking warm sweet drinks. A useful emergency first aid treatment for severe hypothermia is to place the naked patient in a sleeping bag with a naked person of normal temperature.

EYES

Seek immediate medical attention if you develop sudden loss of vision, severe pain in an eye, or have an eye injury.

1. Sore eyes plus mucous discharge

The symptoms of conjunctivitis are gritty, sore eyes on *both sides*, with a discharge especially in the morning, perhaps sticking the eyelids together. Your vision should be normal. You need to bathe the eyes and lids in warm water to remove the mucous discharge. Use antibiotic ointment or drops (e.g. Chloromycetin, Soframycin) four times a day. If there is no improvement in 48 hours see a doctor. This condition is extremely contagious and careful handwashing is essential to ensure it is not spread to others. If you wear contact lenses, these should be removed until the condition has gone away.

2. Sore eyes plus watery discharge

You may be woken in the night by gritty, sore, watering eyes. This could be snow blindness, due to an excess of glare. It could also be called sea blindness – it is common among surfers due to glare *plus* salt water exposure. The treatment is to place a cold compress over the eyes, and take paracetamol with codeine every 4 hours. Eye drops (e.g. Polytears free) may help ease the discomfort. See a doctor if symptoms do not settle in 24 hours. Wear sunglasses.

3. Something (foreign) in the eye

Large particles, splinters, bits of steel etc require urgent specialised medical attention. Do not attempt to remove these, especially if there is any loss of vision. Common grit can be removed safely. You need a good light to see the offending particle. Try and gently wipe the particle away with a clean cloth. If that does not work, flush the eye. Boil half a litre of water and add 1 teaspoon of salt. An empty film canister makes a good eye bath.

If you have no success, the particle could be lodged under the upper eyelid. Enlist a helper to evert the eyelid (turn the underside of the eyelid up and over so you can see it clearly. This sounds dreadful but is painless and often successful! The patient should be seated facing the helper, looking down towards helper's toes.

HELPER: Lay a match stick over the offending eyelid. Grasp the eyelashes of the upper eyelid firmly. Pull upwards over the match stick. Sometimes you need a few attempts. You may not see the offending particle. Wipe the underside of the eyelid with a clean, moist handkerchief. Let go, the patient blinks and the eyelid pops back into place.

EARS

There are several common causes of sore ears in travellers.

1. Tropical Ear

If it is *painful when you pull on the earlobe*, it suggests the outer ear canal walls are inflamed. Tropical Ear is an infection in the outer ear canal. It is common in the tropics, particularly after surfing or repeated swimming. The ear canal becomes waterlogged and germs thrive. There may be a discharge from the ear. Treatment is to take pain killers (e.g. paracetamol) to ease the earache. Place antibiotic cream or drops (e.g. Sofradex, Chloromycetin) into the ear canal. If you must go swimming, keep your head out of the water. Moisture in the outer ear canal will encourage further bacterial growth. Aqua ear can be used to dry the ear after swimming only after the condition has healed.

2. Middle Ear Infection

If *tugging on the ear lobe does not cause pain* - the ear pain is coming from deep inside the ear. The ear pain may be accompanied by a runny nose and/or sore throat. Sometimes hearing may be diminished.

The presence of a temperature above 38°C plus severe ear pain suggests a possible infection in the middle ear space. You need to see a doctor and take antibiotics (e.g. amoxycillin or roxithromycin) to kill the invading bacteria. Painkillers (e.g. paracetamol) may be needed to stop the earache.

If your temperature is normal, it is more likely the middle ear canal is blocked with mucous. Painkillers may be required, but antibiotics are generally not necessary.

3. Pressure Earache

Ear pain *while flying* is commonly due to pressure in the middle ear. Pressure earache may also occur after scuba diving if you are unable to equalise for some reason e.g. you dive with a cold. If you have a pressure earache, you should avoid diving or flying until you get it checked. Take pain killers, decongestants (e.g. Sudafed) or nasal sprays. These will help clear the blockage in your eustacian tubes. For best effect if planning to travel by air, decongestants should be taken half an hour before take off and/or landing.

TEETH AND MOUTH

Loss of a tooth
If a tooth is accidentally knocked out, you need to
- Find the tooth. Handle it only by the crown. If it is dirty, gently rinse it with milk or your own saliva. Do not attempt to clean the tooth by rubbing or using other cleaning agents.
- Gently replace tooth in its socket and seek dental help. If you cannot replace the tooth in its socket, wrap the tooth in cling wrap or plastic while you seek help as quickly as possible.

Gold or porcelain cap (crown) fallen out
Replace the cap to stop the neighbouring teeth closing into the space, and seek dental help.

Broken tooth or filling fallen out
If the tooth is rough and cutting the tongue or cheek, smooth it with an emery board or nail file. Dry the tooth as best you can with a clean handkerchief or tissue. Get a friend to help. Dab the affected area with a cotton bud dipped in oil of cloves or 'toothache drops'. Oil of cloves anaesthetises the nerve in the tooth. If the cavity is large, and you can get hold of some temporary filling preparation (e.g. Cavit), use this as directed to protect the tooth's nerve from damage until you get dental advice.

Tooth pain
Moderate sensitivity and discomfort may be relieved by using oil of cloves as detailed above. If the toothache is severe and the tooth is sore to bite on, it may have an abscess. There may be swelling of the gum near the tooth. Take pain killers and seek dental advice. If dental help will not be available for some days, you may want to start a course of antibiotics (e.g. amoxycillin, roxithromycin) to try to treat the infection.

Gum pain

Sudden onset of gum pain, especially the gum next to a wisdom tooth, is usually due to an infection. Add a teaspoon of salt to a glass of warm (clean) water. Rinse your mouth with this. You should rinse several times per day, especially after eating. Brush as gently as you can. If the gum near the wisdom teeth is infected, you may need to start a course of antibiotics as above, to ease the infection.

Mouth ulcers

Mouth ulcers may be brought on by the stress of travelling. There is a range of mouth ulcer treatments available, but painful ulcers usually respond well to something as simple as regular, warm, salt water rinses. This will prevent secondary infection. Avoid acid foods e.g. pineapple. The ulcer should heal in 2-4 days. If not, see a doctor.

MUSCLES AND JOINTS

1. Injuries

Have your injury reviewed by a doctor as soon as possible. Meanwhile, especially for the first 48 hours, you can help to speed healing by the following:

Rest , Ice, Crepe Bandage, Elevation = "RICE"

Rest

Do not overwork the affected area while it is trying to heal. Give the injury time to heal. The pain is due to torn fibres in your muscles and tendons. If you overuse these torn areas before they heal, you are liable to damage the area more. Return to normal activities gradually.

Ice

Cooling the injured area in the first 24-48 hours will decrease swelling and speed healing. If possible, apply ice wrapped in a towel until the area is cold and feels numb. Remove the ice for 10 to 15 minutes. Keep applying ice on and off even through the night if possible.

Crepe Bandage

This will support the injured area and protect it from further injury. This is especially important if you suspect you have broken a bone.

Always apply a bandage starting at the end of the limb and working towards the trunk. Stretch the bandage slightly as you wrap. Some compression will help decrease swelling, but check it is not so tight it cuts off circulation. Check the fingers and toes are pink. If the upper limb is affected, a sling will help to rest the area.

Elevation
Raise the injured part above the level of the heart to keep swelling to a minimum.

Medication
Anti-inflammatory drugs (e.g. piroxicam, ibuprofen) may be recommended to decrease pain and swelling. These medications are safe provided they are taken with food, for short periods of time, and you do not then overuse the injured muscles and cause further damage.

2. Pains

Muscle and joint pain may occur in association with an illness such as the flu. Paracetamol will provide relief.

BLADDER AND KIDNEYS
(Mostly women)

Infection of the urinary tract usually occurs in women. Take your temperature and look at the urine. An infection will usually cause the urine to become cloudy, discoloured and increase the odour.

Symptoms
Burning or stinging when passing urine usually means cystitis or a urinary tract infection. Sometimes this is accompanied by the feeling of being unable to fully empty the bladder and the need to go to the toilet very frequently e.g. every half an hour.

Treatment
Drink more fluids to 'flush' the germs out of the 'plumbing'. Decrease your coffee intake. Coffee is a kidney stimulant and will make you want to urinate more often. A urinary alkaliniser (e.g. Citravescent or Ural) may help stop the 'burning'. Take one sachet four times a day. Sometimes it is

necessary to take antibiotics to clear the infection. If you cannot get to a doctor the appropriate antibiotics for urinary tract infections are trimethoprim, cotrimoxazole (Bactrim DS) or norfloxacin (Noroxin).

If there is no improvement in 24 hours, you need to see a doctor. Bladder infections may spread upwards to the kidneys which is very serious.

Kidney infections

Watch for the infection spreading to the kidneys. Clues for this are:
* Do you have a fever as well?
* Is there blood in your urine?
* Do you have back pain?

These symptoms raise the definite possibility of kidney infection or Pyelonephritis. You must see a doctor at once.

THRUSH
(Women)

Symptoms

Thrush is a yeast infection of the vagina. The symptoms are a white 'cheesy' discharge, redness of the genital skin, and itch - sometimes quite severe. Thrush is often provoked by being on the contraceptive pill, a course of antibiotics, or some types of malaria pills.

Treatment of thrush

Thrush is easily treated with special creams or pessaries. (e.g. econazole nitrate pessaries - one is placed into the vagina each night for 3 nights.) Other popular treatments are Canesten, Gyno-Daktarin, nystatin, miconazole. If the symptoms do not respond to treatment in a day or two, you must see a doctor urgently as it is probably not thrush. There is also an oral tablet available for severe cases; fluconazole, (Diflucan) one oral dose of 150mg is taken.

EMERGENCY CONTRACEPTION
(Women)

When might it be necessary

For *emergency* use if you have been exposed to the risk of unplanned pregnancy while travelling, and, after careful thought, you wish to avoid an unplanned pregnancy. You will need to have discussed this with your doctor before departure as these medications are only available on prescription.

Emergency contraception may be necessary in the following settings:
- After unprotected intercourse
- After condom or diaphragm mishap
- Rape
- Extreme anxiety about any unprotected intercourse

This emergency contraception (or morning after pill) is only effective when a single act of unprotected intercourse has occurred *within the 72 hours prior to taking medication.* It should never be used repeatedly, or as a 'usual' form of contraception.

How it works

Emergency contraception works in one of two ways. It can prevent ovulation (release of an egg from the ovaries), or it can prevent the fertilised egg from implanting in the womb.

Dosage

Two different medications are required
Nordiol (pink) contraceptive - acts to prevent pregnancy.
Stemetil (yellow) is necessary to prevent vomiting.
The tablets should be taken as follows:
1. take one tablet of prochlorperazine (Stemetil),
2. wait 20 minutes,
3. take two Nordiol tablets with food or a meal.
4. wait 12 hours
5. repeat steps 1-3 above.
For example
10.00*am* one Stemetil; 10.20*am* two Nordiol with food
10.00*pm* one Stemetil; 10.20*pm* two Nordiol with food

If you vomit within 3 hours after dosage, you may need to repeat the Stemetil and Nordiol.

Side effects

You may experience nausea and breast tenderness, also vaginal bleeding may occur in about 4 days time or bleeding may occur at your normal expected period time or your period may be delayed.

See a doctor in four weeks

Although this treatment is very effective, it does not always prevent pregnancy. In any event, you need to see a doctor in 4 weeks. Note that emergency contraception is not recommended for regular contraceptive use.

Condoms (along with water based lubricant) are always necessary to prevent sexually transmitted diseases including AIDS infection.

GENERAL EMERGENCIES

No matter what the emergency, remember.....

Stay Calm   Look For Danger   Call For Help

- Stay calm. You need to accurately assess the situation and carry out any necessary treatment. Treat the most seriously injured first.

- Look for danger - to yourself and the injured person. Many persons have been injured, burned, electrocuted, or hit by cars when trying to assist others. Switch off electricity, gas, motors. Stand well away from fallen power cables (high voltage electricity can jump up to 6 metres and kill you). Make safe any flammable, corrosive or toxic material. Do not let anyone smoke. Do *not* move the casualty unless absolutely necessary, e.g. they are in the path of oncoming cars.

- Call for help from bystanders and emergency services e.g. send a bystander to dial emergency services. You will need to report the location of the emergency, the number and approximate age of the casualties, and the extent of their injuries.

Collapse

If you need to assist a person who has collapsed, first gently shake them and ask 'Are you all right?' If the person does not respond, remember the ABC.

AIRWAY   **B**REATHING   **C**IRCULATION

Airway

When treating an unconscious casualty, the first priority is to ensure a clear airway so they can breathe. Laying the person flat on their back may cause airway obstruction and death. Place the person on their left side, with right knee resting on the ground in front, and right hip and knee joints at right angles. This is called the Lateral Recovery Position.

LATERAL RECOVERY POSITION

Support the person's head and neck while moving them. With their head on the side, use your fingers to gently clear the mouth of any food, fluids or loose dentures.

Keep the face tilted slightly downwards, so fluids can drain from their mouth. Check to see if they are breathing.

Breathing

If the person is not breathing, they need mouth-to-mouth resuscitation. Make a note of the time as you start resuscitation. Gently roll the casualty onto their back. Place one hand holding their chin, tilt their head backwards, support the jaw and keep your fingers away from their throat. With the other hand, pinch their nostrils together, open your mouth wide and seal your lips around the casualty's mouth. Blow into their mouth until the chest rises. (For small children cover their nose and mouth with your mouth and puff gently.)

Listen for air escaping from the nose and mouth. Watch the chest to see if it rises and falls. Give five full breaths as quickly as possible. Pause and check the pulse – the carotid pulse is usually easiest. If their heart is beating, continue giving **one breath every 4 seconds**

If spontaneous breathing begins, place the casualty in the recovery position.

Circulation

If the pulse is absent, external cardiac compression may be necessary to help keep the blood circulating to the brain until help arrives. *Ideally you should be trained to do this effectively.*

In an emergency, the heel of the hand is placed on the lower half of the breastbone, you press down about 5cm (2 inches) with each compression. The rhythm should be..

Single rescuer	2 breaths to 15 compressions
Two rescuers	1 breath to 5 compressions

Check the casualty's pulse every 2 minutes, while you wait for help.

If you feel a pulse, stop cardiac compression immediately.

CHILD TRAVELLERS' FIRST AID

The first aid instructions described previously are intended for adults. Some listed medications are not suitable for children.

This section is short because if children are sick they *must* be taken to a competent doctor. Self-treatment is really for adults only. Children get *sicker faster.* Their reserves are smaller, and their immune system is immature. Giving antibiotics to sick children without medical advice is especially dangerous. If your child becomes ill, you need to seek medical advice without delay. Meanwhile to assess the severity of their illness you need to:

1. Take their temperature. Normal is 37°C. It is very serious if a child develops a fever persistently over 39°C. Regular paracetamol and sponging with tepid water (left to evaporate off their skin) may help to bring a child's temperature down while you seek medical attention. If the child has visited a malarious area, it could be malaria. Malaria may be rapidly fatal in children if it is not treated.

2. Check their pulse rate. The normal pulse rate for children is 80 -100 beats per minute and for infants 100-140 beats per minute. A raised pulse rate is usually a sign of significant illness.

3. Are they eating and more importantly, drinking? If a child is eating normally, it is a good sign that they are not too sick. If they lose their appetite, but are still drinking fluids, they can hold their own. If they stop drinking fluids it is very serious. If a child is not passing urine in normal amounts, they must be taken to medical care urgently. Children dehydrate much more quickly than adults.

Diarrhoea in children

A study of traveller's diarrhoea among Swiss travellers showed that the highest incidence, severest disease and longest duration of traveller's diarrhoea occurred in travellers under the age of three. If children get diarrhoea, they should *not* be starved. Babies should continue breast feeding or formula *plus* be given oral rehydration fluids (e.g. Gastrolyte). Older children should be given starchy foods e.g. cooked rice, maize, wheat (toast), or potatoes. Bananas are also useful to supply needed potassium. Children who are dehydrated should not be given soft drinks as it may make their dehydration worse - soft drinks contain too much sugar and not enough potassium and salt.

DRUG REFERENCE TABLE

Name	Use	Other Names & Strength	Dose	Precautions

It is best to check with the doctor before departure regarding the suitability to take medication, especially if you are on any medication already e.g. for hypertension, epilepsy, diabetes, mental illness etc. This table does not replace good medical advice.
Trade names are in **bold** type, and generic or worldwide names are in normal type.

Name	Use	Other Names & Strength	Dose	Precautions
Acetazolamide	Speeds adaptation to altitude Take either 1. Before exposure to prevent mild symptoms of altitude sickness. or 2. To treat mild symptoms of altitude sickness	Acetazolamide 250 mg tablets. = **Diamox**	Take half a 250 mg tablet (ie 125mg) every 12 hours. 1. For prevention start 2 days before reaching 2700m. or 2. For treatment start when you get symptoms. See pages 64-66 Max 2 tabs/day	Do not take if allergic to sulphur drugs. Possible side effects are tingling sensation in feet or hands, loss of appetite, and a flat taste of carbonated drinks. Some people notice decreased tolerance to exercise.
Amoxycillin	Antibiotic for chest, sinus, middle ear or dental infections	Amoxycillin 250mg or 500mg (bigger dose if illness is more severe) **Amoxil** = **Moxacin**	One every 8 hours for 5 days. Must finish the course.	Should not be taken if allergic to penicillin. They can be taken with food.
Antihistamine There are many different ones	For relief of allergies e.g. hayfever, or insect bites. Also used for motion sickness and some types are used for sedation.	e.g **Avil Claratyne Hismanal Polaramine Teldane Telfast Zadine Zyrtec**	Doses are different for each one e.g. **Teldane** is one tablet twice a day, **Zyrtec** is once a day. See promethazine For motion sickness doses	Some of the older antihistamines can cause drowsiness. Do not drink alcohol or operate machinery while using them. **Teldane** should not be used if taking erythromycin or roxithromycin.
Avomine		See promethazine		
Bactrim DS	Antibiotic used to treat infection of chest, throat, middle ear, skin and bladder infections. Also cyclospora diarrhoea – see page 92	Cotrimoxazole = Trimethoprim 160mg plus Sulpha - methoxazole 800mg = **Septrin Forte**	Take one tablet morning and evening, after meals, for 5 days.	A sulphur drug, so it should not be taken by those with sulphur allergies. Cease drug immediately if rash develops.
Biltricide		See praziqantel		
Buscopan	Antispasmodic - To treat stomach cramps	Hyoscine butylbromide 10mg	Take 20mg (2 tablets) four times a day	Take the dose prescribed; it doesn't work well at lower doses.

DRUG REFERENCE TABLE

Name	Use	Other Names & Strength	Dose	Precautions
Cephalexin	Antibiotic for treatment of wound infections.	Cephalexin 250mg or 500mg **Keflex, Ibilex** (cephalosporin family)	Usually 500mg twice a day Can take up to 4g per day	This family of drugs have some similarities to penicillin family, so those with penicillin allergies sometimes react to this.
Chloromycetin ointment or drops	Antibiotic ointment or drops for conjunctivitis. Can also be used in emergency for external ear infections ie. 'tropical ear'.	**Chloram-phenicol**	Apply ointment or drops every four hours for 2 to 3 days.	Chloramphenicol *tablets* should only be used under medical supervision, but drops or ointment are much safer. Do not use on the ear if eardrum is perforated.
Chloroquine	Anti-malarial Usually used for prevention of malaria and occasionally for treatment of malaria in chloroquine sensitive areas.	**Aralen Avlochlor Nivaquine Resochin Chlorquin** Usually 150 mg of chloroquine base in each tablet	To prevent malaria take two tablets per week, e.g. two tablets every Monday. Start two weeks before exposure, take two tablets each week while in the risk area, and keep taking until 4 weeks after leaving the risk area. See page 18. For treatment dose see page 83.	Must be taken with food and plenty of water. Chloroquine tablets taste very bitter as they are similar to the quinine in tonic water. Some countries e.g. UK can supply coated (tasteless) tablets Some people notice blurry vision, nausea, headaches.
Ciprofloxacin	Antibiotic for diarrhoea, chest infection wound infections	Ciprofloxacin 500mg tablets = **Ciproxin** or **Cipro**	For treatment of diarrhoea take two 500mg tablets (total 1 g) at once For chest or wound infections take one 500mg tablet three times a day.	Very expensive in Australia, but commonly used overseas.
Ciproxin	See Ciprofloxacin above			
Coloxyl	Laxative - eases constipation.	Docusate sodium 120 mg tabs	Two coloxyl each night after your evening meal.	Also drink more fluids, eat more fibre and get more exercise.

DRUG REFERENCE TABLE

Name	Use	Other Names & Strength	Dose	Precautions
Cotrimoxazole	See Bactrim DS			
Diamox	See Acetazolamide			
Diflucan	See Fluconazole			
Dimen-hydrinate	Motion sickness	**Drammamine** tablets and syrup Adult 50mg tab Junior 25mg tab Syrup 2.5mg/ml	Adult One tablet 3-4 times a day Children's dose 2-3 times daily 2-6yrs ; 6.25 –12.5mg 6-8yrs 12.5-25mg 8-12 yrs; 25-50mg >12 years 50mg	Side effects are drowsiness and dizziness. In children there can be excitement. Need for frequent administration.
Diphenoxylate HCl	See Lomotil			
Doxycycline	1. Anti-malarial or 2. Antibiotic for chest infections or some skin infections.	Doxycycline is available in 50mg or 100mg strengths. 100mg capsules or tablets are most common. Also known as **Doryx** or **Vibramycin**	To prevent malaria take 100 mg per day with food, see p 18. To treat chest & other susceptible infections; take one tablet morning and night on the first day, then one tablet daily after that for 6 days. Always take with food and fluid & do not lie down for several hours.	If taken on an empty stomach, it will cause heart-burn. Sun sensitivity can develop. Women may develop thrush and doxy-cycline may occasionally interfere with the effectiveness of the contraceptive pill. Avoid anticoagulants, penicillins and antacids while on doxycycline.
Econazole	For treatment of fungal infections or thrush.	Econazole Nitrate 150mg cream or ovules = **Pevaryl**	Apply cream or Insert 1 pessary nightly for 3 nights.	See a doctor if symptoms persist.
Fansidar	For treatment of malaria in some countries.	Sulphadoxine 500mg + 25mg Pyrimethamine	Take three tablets all together.	Should not be taken if you have sulphur allergies.
Fasigyn	see Tinidazole			
Fluconazole	For treatment of severe vaginal thrush.	Fluconazole 150mg= **Diflucan**	Take one tablet orally.	Occasional side effects nausea, abdominal pain, headache

DRUG REFERENCE TABLE

Name	Use	Other Names & Strength	Dose	Precautions
Flucloxacillin	Antibiotic for treatment of skin infections, e.g. infected coral cuts.	Flucloxacillin 250 mg or 500mg capsules = **Flopen**	Take one capsule every 6 hours, (one hour before meals) for 6 days.	Should not be taken if allergic to penicillin or history of liver disease. Rarely causes hepatitis.
Gastrolyte	Essential salts and sugars in a balanced formula for increased gut absorption of water. For all types of diarrhoea and vomiting, to treat dehydration.	Each 4.9g sachet contains NaCl (salt) 470mg, KCl (potassium) 300mg, Na acid citrate 530mg, glucose 3.56g.	For one dose, mix one sachet of gastrolyte with 200mls of boiled or purified water - preferably in the measuring cup provided. Drink one dose after each vomit or loose motion.	Gastrolyte is safe for children. Take small sips regularly. If you are unable to keep down enough fluids to balance what you are losing, seek medical help immediately.
Hyoscine hydrobromide	See **Kwells**			
Hyoscine butylbromide	See **Buscopan**			
Ibuprofen	Pain killer and anti - inflammatory medication	Ibuprofen 200mg = **Nurofen**	Take one to two tablets every 4 hours as necessary. WITH FOOD	Maximum of six tablets per day. May interfere with some blood pressure and heart medication. Should be used with care if there is a history of asthma, esp. if not previously used or if known allergy to aspirin. May cause indigestion.
Imodium	See Loperamide			
Iodine tablets	Water purification	Iodine tablets (also available as a liquid, but tablets are less messy)	Add 1 tablet to 1 litre of water and leave to stand for 30 minutes. If the water is very cold, you may need up to 60 minutes. see p 44-45	Tastes bad. Avoid this if you have an allergy to iodine or seafood, or if you have thyroid disease. If you take the solution and the bottle leaks, it will destroy your clothes and metal items.

DRUG REFERENCE TABLE

Name	Use	Other Names & Strength	Dose	Precautions
Kwells	Motion sickness	Hyoscine hydrobromide 0.3mg	Take 30 minutes before travel. Repeat in 4-6 hours if needed. Adult 1-2 tablets max 4 in 24 hrs Children 2-7 years 1/4 tab max 1 tab in 24 hrs >7 years 1/2 to 1 tab , max 2 tabs in 24 hrs	Common side effects are dry mouth, blurry vision, and drowsiness.
Lariam	See Mefloquine			
Lomotil	Anti-diarrhoea. A 'stopper' – i.e. paralyses the bowel – for when diarrhoea is inconvenient.	Diphenoxylate HCl 2.5 mg, and atropine sulfate 25mcg	Take two tablets 3-4 times a day for a maximum of 48 hours.	Do not take if you have a fever or blood in the bowel motions.
Loperamide	Anti - diarrhoea pill. A 'stopper' for temporary relief of symptoms when diarrhoea is inconvenient. Very useful if no toilets available e.g. on a raft or bus.	Loperamide HCl 2mg = **Imodium** = **Gastrostop**	Two capsules at once, then one after each loose bowel motion. Maximum 8 capsules per day for 48 hours. see p 83-91 for full discussion of diarrhoea treatment	Remember diarrhoea is a natural defence mechanism. Do not take this if you have a fever or blood in the motion - the germs will be held inside and the diarrhoea may get worse.
Malarone	Malaria treatment in drug resistant areas. (Also very occasionally used for prevention of malaria see p18)	Atovoquone 25mg plus Proguanil 100mg	For treatment the dose is taken each day for 3 consecutive days Adults – 4 tabs daily – total of 12 Children Dosage per day 11-20kg - 1 tab 21-30kg - 2 tabs 31-40kg - 3 tabs >40kg - 4 tablets	Not to be used under 3 years of age. No major side effects are described.
Maloprim	Anti-malarial Often given in combination with chloroquine.	Pyrimethamine 12.5mg, Dapsone 100mg	One tablet per week, from 2 weeks before until 4 weeks after risk area.	Rarely causes bone marrow failure so is no longer used.

DRUG REFERENCE TABLE

Name	Use	Other Names & Strength	Dose	Precautions
Maxolon	Anti-nausea	Metoclopramide 10mg	After you have emptied the contents of your stomach, take one tablet. Take one tablet every 8 hours.	If nausea persists or the vomiting is continuous for more than 24 hours, dehydration can occur rapidly. See a doctor.
Mebendazole	Anti-worm pill	Mebendazole 100mg tablets = **Vermox**	Take one tablet morning and night for three days (total of 6 tablets) on return from overseas areas where 'worms' are common.	
Mefloquine	1. Prevention of malaria 2. Standby (emergency) treatment of fevers in case it is malaria, when medical advice is not available.	Mefloquine 250mg tablets = **Lariam**	1. For prevention: One tablet per week, start 4 weeks before entering risk area, take one tablet per week while at risk and continue until 4 weeks after return. 2. Standby treatment of malaria - take 2 tablets to start, and a further one to two tablets in six hours. For detailed information on treatment of fevers - see p81.	Take with food or plenty of fluid. May cause strange dreams, dizziness, disturbed balance, or gut upset. Avoid heavy alcohol within 24 hours of dose. Not advised in persons with epilepsy, mental illness, pilots, those taking beta-blockers, or digoxin. Avoid pregnancy for 3 months after Lariam.
Metronidazole	Antibiotic for diarrhoea germs: Giardia or Amoebic Dysentery	Metronidazole 200mg or 400mg tablets = **Flagyl**	Take 400mg three times a day for 7 days.	No alcohol must be taken during or for 2 days after course. Do not take with anti-epilepsy or some anti-ulcer drugs e.g. **Tagamet.**

DRUG REFERENCE TABLE

Name	Use	Other Names & Strength	Dose	Precautions
Norfloxacin	Antibiotic for 1. bacterial diarrhoea or 2. bladder infections	Norfloxacin 400mg tablets = **Noroxin**	For faster action; Take two 2 tablets to start, then one every 12 hours to total of 6 tablets. Usual dose is one tab every 12 hours for 3 days. Take one hour before or two hours after food.	Avoid antacids and multivitamin preparations containing zinc while taking Norfloxacin. They may decrease the absorption of Norfloxacin from the stomach.
Paludrine	Prevent malaria in certain areas. (Combined with Atovoquone it may be used for treatment of malaria see Malarone.)	Proguanil 100mg tablets	Take two tablets per day, starting 2 weeks before entering the malarious area, take while there and for 4 weeks after malaria area.	May cause mouth ulcers, rash, headache, dizziness.
Paracetamol	Pain killer	Paracetamol 500 mg = **Panadol** = **Dymadon**	Take two every four hours.	See a doctor if pain persists. Maximum of eight tabs per day.
Paracetamol with codeine	Stronger pain killer	Paracetamol 500mg plus Codeine 8mg = **Panadeine**	Take two every four hours.	Maximum of eight tablets per day. See doctor if pain persists.
Pevaryl	See Econazole			
Phenergan	See Promethazine			
Praziquantel	Treat proven schistosomiasis.	Praziquantel 600mg = **Biltricide**	Take dose (20mg per kg body weight) 3 times daily (every four hours) for 1 day.	Swallow whole with liquid after meals.
Proguanil	See **Paludrine** And **Malarone**			
Promethazine	Motion sickness	**Phenergan Avomine** 25mg tabs	Take dose each night, starting the night before travel. Dose <u>Adult</u> - 1 tablet <u>Children</u> 3-5yrs; 1/4 tab 5-10yrs; 1/2 tab	For short journeys start 2 hours before departure. It causes marked drowsiness. Caffeine may counter the drowsiness. Avoid alcohol.

DRUG REFERENCE TABLE

Name	Use	Other Names & Strength	Dose	Precautions
Quinine	For treatment of malaria	Quinine 300mg tablets	2 tabs = 600mg three times a day for 7 days. May be taken with Fansidar or Doxycycline	Side effects are nausea, vomiting headache, ringing in ears and muffled hearing.
Roxithromycin	Antibiotic for chest infections or skin infections or dental infections.	Roxithromycin 150mg or 300mg tablets = **Rulide** = **Biaxsig** (a type of erythromycin)	Take 300mg once a day, at least 15 minutes before food, for 5 days.	3% of persons taking this will get abdominal pain, nausea, or diarrhoea. Do not take with **Teldane** or **Hismanal.**
Rulide	See roxithromycin above			
SCOP	Skin patch to prevent motion sickness.	Hyoscine 1.5mg	Apply to dry undamaged, hairless skin behind your ear, 6-8 hours before the journey. Effective for 72 hours.	Side effects may be dry mouth, blurred vision and drowsiness. Avoid alcohol. Remove patch for a few hours if you get side effects. Do not take if under 12 or over 65 years of age.
Septrin Forte	See Bactrim DS			
Stemetil	Anti-nausea Wait for stomach contents to empty before taking this	Prochlorperazine maleate Tablets 5mg or Suppositories 25mg	*Tablets* One or two tablets every 8 to 12 hours. *Suppository* One rectally and follow with tablet 6 hours later	If vomiting continues dehydration can occur rapidly. Do not take for more than 24 hours without seeing a doctor.
Sudafed	Clears runny nose especially if travelling on aeroplanes.	Pseudoephedrine 60mg	One tablet 30 minutes before take off and landing. Limit of 3 per day.	Do not take if you have a tendency to raised blood pressure.
Temazepam	Mild sleeping pill Works for about 4 hours -very useful on planes.	Temazepam 10mg = **Euhypnos** = **Normison**	1-2 tablets, 30 minutes before you wish to sleep.	Do not take with other tranquillisers or more than one glass of alcohol.
Tinidazole	Antibiotic for diarrhoea germs; 1. Giardia or 2. Amoebic Dysentery.	Tinidazole 500mg tablets = **Fasigyn** = **Simplotan** **Tiniba** is also in this family of drugs	1. Giardia - take 4 tabs with food. 2. For Amoebic dysentery, take 4 tablets together with food *each day for 3 days,* (total 12 tablets).	No alcohol must be taken for 2 days after dose. Some people notice headache, rash, or metallic taste in the mouth after tinidazole.

A FEW DETAILS

AIDS

What is it?
AIDS (Acquired Immunodeficiency Syndrome) is caused by infection with a virus known as the Human Immunodeficiency Virus (HIV). This virus attacks the immune system - the body's natural defence against infections - and causes it to slow down and eventually fail. AIDS is the end result of infection with HIV. Infections the body would normally fight off, can be fatal. If a person is infected with HIV, and has not yet developed AIDS, they will be infectious to others, and yet look and feel perfectly well. Occasionally a person may have a negative AIDS test and yet be infectious to others. The blood test measures antibodies to the HIV. It may take three months after first contact for those antibodies to develop.

How it is spread?
The HIV virus is delicate and cannot survive outside the body. It must travel person-to-person in body fluids. HIV does not spread through normal social contact between friends, workmates or family members. You cannot catch HIV from shaking hands, hugging, coughing, sitting next to someone, or from cutlery or plates. Mosquitoes do not transmit HIV, (the virus cannot survive in the insect's gut). You catch HIV from sexual contact, blood products, sharing infected needles and syringes. Since the onset of the epidemic 15 years ago, the virus has infected more than 47 million people in the world. AIDS led to more than 2.2 million deaths in 1998. Over 95% of all cases and AIDS deaths occur in the developing world, mostly among young adults and increasingly in women.

CHAGAS DISEASE

Chagas disease is a potentially fatal parasitic infection of the heart and gut. It is transmitted via cone-nosed bugs in the Americas - especially rural Brazil. The bugs live in the walls of mud huts, and come out at night for a blood meal. While feeding, the parasites (trypanosomes) are excreted onto the victim's skin via the faeces of the bug. Unsuspecting victims scratch these parasites into the bite wound. Early symptoms are swelling around the bite, followed by swelling of the lymph glands and/or a fever. Later complications include damage to the heart (causing sudden death), and paralysis of the gut (causing constipation and difficulty swallowing.) Treatment is difficult, so prevention is best – do not sleep inside mud huts (adobes) in the Americas. It is best to camp some distance away. Visitors to large cities or to remote jungle ruins are not at risk.

CHOLERA

This disease causes a sudden onset of extremely profuse, watery diarrhoea one to two days after contact with the germ. The diarrhoea is completely painless but large amounts of fluid can be lost in a short time e.g. one litre every few hours. This leads to rapid dehydration if the fluids and salts are not replaced. With proper treatment the disease lasts two days, and the person recovers completely. Cholera is rare in tourists but common in malnourished people, especially children. In areas where there are no medical facilities, cholera may be severe, and 60% of infected children may die. Cholera is caused by a bacteria (Vibrio cholera) and transmitted via contaminated water or food.

Recently a new strain of cholera has appeared. It is called the O139 strain or 'Bengal' cholera. The most commonly used vaccine is not very effective anyway, and does not work against the new strain. The best way to prevent cholera is to be extremely careful what you eat and drink. A new oral cholera vaccine is now available. It is very effective but does not prevent the new O139. Cholera is such a rare disease in tourists, the vaccine is seldom necessary.

CIGUATERA

Ciguatera fish poisoning has been known for centuries, mainly in the tropical and subtropical Pacific and Indian Ocean regions and the tropical Caribbean. Up to 50,000 people worldwide suffer from the disease annually. It develops after eating fish containing ciguatera toxins. These toxins arise from a type of marine algae found near coral, and are concentrated in the muscles of the fish that eat the algae. The higher up the food chain (the bigger the fish) the more concentrated the toxin, and the more severe the symptoms. Local fishermen are often aware of the high-risk species. The toxin is difficult to detect - contaminated fish taste normal. Cooking does not destroy the toxin. Symptoms vary but usually begin with gut discomfort within hours of eating the fish. Within 24 hours other symptoms start to develop including tingling or strange sensations in the limbs and around the mouth. Hot things may feel cold or vice versa. Muscle and joint pains, weakness, itchiness, sweating, and even hallucinations have been described. Symptoms may persist for months or years. People who have previously had ciguatera may suffer a recurrence of typical symptoms after eating fish that do not cause symptoms in others. The favoured treatment at present is intravenous mannitol, so medical advice must be sought.

DENGUE FEVER

Dengue is present in many parts of the world, even occasionally in North Queensland. See map below.

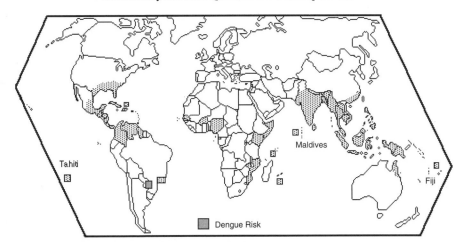

How do you catch Dengue Fever?
It is spread from person-to-person by a mosquito (Aedes aegypti) which bites during the day. If you have a snooze during the day you are especially at risk.

What are the symptoms of Dengue?
About 1 week after the bite, a mild runny nose develops, followed a few hours later by the sudden onset of fever, a splitting headache, and severe muscle and joint pains. After 2 to 3 days the fever and pains settle. The apparent recovery may only last 2 days, then symptoms return, though less severely. Small red spots may appear on the trunk and spread to face and limbs. There is no treatment. After a few more days the fever subsides and full recovery follows. Although an unpleasant illness, serious complications are rare from the first attack. It is common to be tired for weeks afterwards. Immunity after an attack is not lifelong. There are four strains of the dengue virus. If you are exposed to a different strain at a later time, the second attack is likely to be more serious than the first. It can cause Dengue Shock which leads to excessive bleeding and a serious drop in blood pressure. This needs to be treated in a good hospital.

How can I avoid Dengue Fever?
There is no vaccine. The best protection is to avoid mosquitoes.

DIPHTHERIA

Diphtheria bacteria infect the throat and release a poison which paralyses the heart and nervous system.

You catch the disease by breathing in contaminated droplets from the air (like the common cold). Although it occurs worldwide, it is especially common in developing countries. Recently there was a huge outbreak of diphtheria in the old 'Russia'. Vaccination is recommended for all travellers, but diphtheria is most serious in the very young and the elderly. Diphtheria vaccination is usually combined with tetanus. It can also be given on its own if you have had a recent Tetanus vaccination but no recent Diphtheria vaccine.

FLU

The influenza virus causes fever, cough, aches and pains, headache and extreme tiredness. Sometimes there is also a sore throat and clear discharge from the nose. Fever usually lasts 1-5 days but cough and tiredness may persist for one to two weeks. An individual can sneeze the virus a distance of three metres, and the flu is caught from these particles in the air. Symptoms develop about 1-2 days after first contact with the virus. Sufferers need to rest and take paracetamol. Most people will recover fully.

Influenza vaccination is recommended for persons over 65 as they are more likely to develop complications after the flu such as bronchitis or pneumonia. Other travellers may benefit from a flu vaccine. Influenza occurs year round in the tropics. Travellers are more prone to the flu as they are often exposed to crowds (and hence more viruses) on aeroplanes, in shopping centres and at historic sights. Crowded bus tours are particularly good environments for spreading the virus. A traveller's immune system may be weakened by eating poorly, drinking too much alcohol, not getting enough rest, and rapidly crossing time zones and climate zones e.g. from summer to winter in the space of a day. Furthermore, in the event of illness, travellers are a long way from their usual doctor, and their own bed. This makes the illness more uncomfortable and complications more likely.

The flu vaccine is about 80% effective against the current strains of the flu. The vaccine changes every year because the virus does too.

The Flu vaccine is a dead vaccine so it is impossible for the Flu vaccine to give you a dose of the Flu. After vaccination, it takes about 2 weeks for immunity to develop. During this two weeks you can still catch the Flu. The vaccine also cannot prevent the common cold.

HEPATITIS OVERVIEW

Hepatitis means infection of the liver. There are many types of hepatitis: A, B, C, D, E, F and G at last count. Hepatitis may also occur as part of another illness such as Glandular Fever, or as a side effect from a drug.

Vaccines are only currently available against Hepatitis A (contracted from food), and Hepatitis B (contracted from blood products). Hepatitis C is transmitted via blood transfusions. Hepatitis D can only occur with Hepatitis B. Hepatitis E is caught from food and water, like Hepatitis A, and is particularly serious in pregnant women.

HEPATITIS A

Three to four weeks after contact with infected food or water, the sufferer develops a fever. This is accompanied by loss of appetite, stomach discomfort and yellowing of the whites of the eyes and skin. The urine becomes dark and the motions become pale. On average, the sufferer loses a month off work, and alcohol may not allowed for up to one year. In adults, Hepatitis A can cause tiredness for months afterwards. The disease is seldom fatal, though it is more likely to be fatal in persons over 40 years of age.

This disease is common in third world countries because sanitation is poor. In developing countries most locals contract the disease in childhood. Once someone has had Hepatitis A they cannot catch it again. Hepatitis A is also known as 'Yellow Jaundice'. This type is quite different to baby jaundice. Baby jaundice is caused by immaturity of the liver and develops in the first few days of life.

Adult travellers to developing countries should be vaccinated against Hepatitis A.

Backpackers are more prone to Hepatitis A (about one case per 50 backpackers per month of stay). Travellers staying in five star hotels are not always safe however.

Hepatitis A is usually extremely mild in young children, and if they contract the disease they are immune for life. For this reason, vaccination is not usually recommended for children under 2 years of age.

Protection against Hepatitis A can be given as either:
1. Vaqta / Havrix. These excellent manufactured vaccines give long term protection with few side effects, but are more expensive. Twinrix gives long term protection against hepatitis A and B
2. Gamma Globulin. - also known as Immune Globulin. This is a blood product. It has been used safely for 50 years. It has been carefully investigated and shown not to transmit AIDS or Hepatitis B, but cannot be proven 100% safe from diseases as yet undiscovered. It is less effective than the 'real vacines' - there have been cases of persons developing severe Hepatitis A disease, despite recent Gamma Globulin. Protection lasts a shorter time. The only slight advantage over Vaqta and Havrix is that it is cheaper.

HEPATITIS B

The disease Hepatitis B causes symptoms of tiredness, nausea, loss of appetite, rash, muscle and joint pains. Symptoms develop two to six months after exposure to the virus. The skin and whites of the eyes turn yellow, the urine may become tea coloured and the bowel motions turn whitish. The acute illness lasts several weeks. 1.4% of sufferers will die during the acute attack. 6-10% of adult sufferers remain chronically infected or infectious to others, and one fifth of those chronically infected will die from the infection. Chronic Hepatitis B carriers are 94 times more likely than average to develop a primary liver cancer.

Hepatitis B virus is fragile and cannot survive long outside the body. It must travel from person to person through blood or other body fluids i.e. transfusions, sharing contaminated needles or sexual contact (similar to AIDS). Acupuncture, tattoos, dental procedures can also transmit the disease. It is present all over the world, including Australia, but is more prevalent in developing countries.

Travellers anticipating sexual contacts overseas should be vaccinated. Vaccination is also recommended for long-term travellers to developing countries (greater than 3 months), and for those working with blood or blood products.

Children may be at risk if they play with infected children. Minor injuries are common during play and the virus could pass from one to the other via broken skin. The National Health and Medical Research Council of Australia now includes Hepatitis B vaccination with all the other 'standard' childhood vaccines.

Note that the Hepatitis B virus and the Hepatitis A virus are very different. Vaccination against one does not protect you from infection with the other, however there is now a combined vaccine (Twinrix) which does give protection from both.

JAPANESE B ENCEPHALITIS

Japanese B Encephalitis (JE) is a viral disease spread by the bite of a particular mosquito (culex). This mosquito breeds in rice paddies and picks up the infection when feeding on pigs and wading birds. For this reason, the disease mainly occurs in rural/farming areas. JE is present in rural areas of China, India, Sri Lanka, Nepal, Burma, Thailand, Laos, Vietnam, Korea, and the Philippines. Cases have recently been reported from the Torres Strait and Papua New Guinea. These days JE is seldom a problem in Japan. Patterns of JE transmission vary regionally, depending on rainfall (worse during summer monsoons) and other factors from year to year.

The culex mosquito bites mostly at dusk, dawn and on cloudy days. In affected areas, some studies have shown only 3% of culex mosquitoes carry the virus. However, in affected areas, almost everyone has been exposed to the JE virus by the age of 15. Roughly 99.5% of those exposed to the virus do not get sick. If sickness does develop, the virus infects the brain leading to fevers, headache and encephalitis. 25% of those who get sick will die and 30% will be left with permanent brain damage.

Worldwide, approximately 50,000 cases of JE are reported annually, however the risk to most travellers is very low. Vaccination would generally be recommended for travellers who will be living long term in affected areas, travelling repeatedly to risky areas or visiting areas where there is an outbreak in progress.

The risk of side effects from the JE Vaccine are as follows
- 20% experience effects *at* the site of injection such as tenderness, redness, or swelling of the arm

- 10% experience effects *away from* the site of injection such as fever, headache, malaise, rash, nausea, vomiting, muscle aches, abdominal pain.
- 0.1-1% experience more severe allergic reactions to the vaccine - rash, allergic swelling (of the lips, face, limbs and joints), low blood pressure or dizziness. Rarely, life threatening breathing difficulties have been reported.

If an allergic reaction is to occur it may occur after any of the three doses. If it occurs after the first dose, it is usually about 12 hours later and 88% will occur within 3 days.

If it occurs after the second or third dose, it is usually 3 days later but may be as much as 10 days. Hence the course of JE Vax must be completed 10 days before departure. Some people cannot be vaccinated for medical reasons. JE is yet another reason to diligently avoid mosquito bites.

KALA AZAR

What is it?
Visceral leishmaniasis or kala azar is a disease which causes fevers, weakness, stomach and muscle pains, loss of appetite, diarrhoea, and constipation. It may mimic malaria with a sudden onset of high fevers. After months of infection, the skin will become grey and scaly. Kala azar means 'black disease'. Eventually the sufferer becomes susceptible to infections (like AIDS victims) and dies. Kala azar is known in some countries as Black Fever (not related to the Black Plague). Kala azar is found in Africa, South America, Middle East, Asia (especially India), China and occasionally in Europe.

How do you catch Kala azar?
It is transmitted by the bite of infected female sandflies. The sandfly breeds in rubbish or cracks in walls. Sandflies are very tiny and can fly through most mosquito nets.

How do you avoid Kala azar?
Although the risk to travellers is low, there is no vaccine or preventative drugs. Campers and backpackers are more at risk. Avoid known infected areas, wear protective clothing and regularly use insect repellent containing DEET.

MALARIA

Each year about 900 people return to Australia with this unwelcome souvenir of their travels. The following map gives you some idea where malaria occurs.

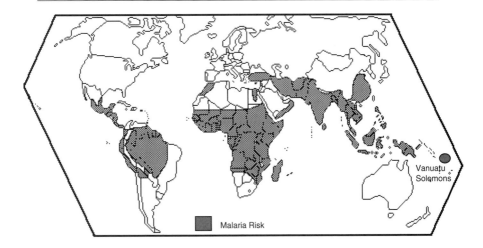

Malaria Risk

We do not know exactly how many people are infected worldwide. Disease estimates in third world countries are notoriously unreliable. WHO (the World Health Organisation) estimates that there are at least 110 million new cases, and about 1 million people die each year. A large proportion of these deaths occur among children in Africa.

History

Hippocrates first described the disease in 400BC. It was not until the mid 1600's that the first cure was found. The Countess of Chinchon was cured of malaria by an infusion from the bark of a fever tree (afterwards called the Chinchona tree).

The infusion became popular for all sorts of feverish illnesses. It was given mixed with claret. As you can imagine, this treatment did not cure everyone's fevers but perhaps it cheered up the sufferers.

Though we know a great deal about the malaria parasite, there are many logistical problems in eradicating malaria.

The life cycle of Malaria

There are four strains of malarial parasite. The most serious form is *falciparum*. It causes cerebral malaria and can be fatal. Falciparum parasites attack *all* the body's red blood cells. The other types of malaria: *vivax, ovale* and *malariae* attack only the very old or young red cells so there are many cells left to carry oxygen. For this reason *vivax, ovale* and *malariae* infections are usually less serious.

Malaria parasites enter the blood via the bite of an infected mosquito. The parasites travel to the liver and invade individual liver cells. During the next one to two weeks each parasite multiplies up to 40,000 times within its liver cell. (The sufferer feels well during this incubation period.) Eventually, parasite numbers increase so much, they cause their liver cell to burst, releasing parasites into the blood. Once in the blood stream the parasites invade the oxygen transporters - the red blood cells.

Malaria parasites feed on the contents of their red blood cell and multiply many times. That red cell eventually bursts releasing a shower of more parasites into the blood stream which attack more red cells. Symptoms (fevers and chills) develop at this stage. Every time a red blood cell bursts, many more parasites are released to attack more red blood cells. The parasite numbers can increase very rapidly. See Graph 1 which shows a fictional attack of malaria.

The *vivax* and *ovale* strains may have a long liver phase so they may not produce symptoms for many months. This is why you need a blood test for malaria even if you develop fevers *many months* after leaving the malaria risk area.

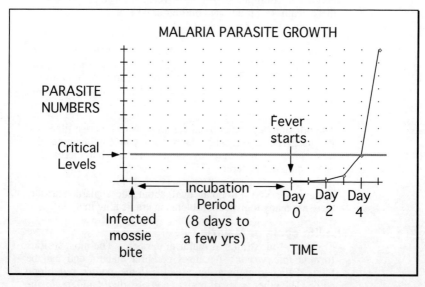

Graph 1

The shortest recorded time between getting a malaria fever and being brain dead is 60 hours.

It is vital to treat malaria as early as possible. Full recovery is possible if malaria is treated in the early stages. If the disease progresses however, complications develop. At this late stage, killing the parasites may not be enough to save the patient. Dead parasites and red cell debris block tiny blood vessels, especially those of the brain, causing cerebral malaria.

Medication

Tablets to prevent malaria have only been available since World War Two. Today's tablets are a big improvement over 'an infusion from the bark of a fever tree mixed with claret'. There are definitely fewer side effects for a start.

There are now many different malaria tablets with different actions and side effects. They are taken daily or weekly, alone or in combination. Unfortunately, however, none of the tablets available are perfectly safe and perfectly effective. Some are safer than others. Different areas of the world may require different tablets to prevent malaria.

Drug resistance is a grave problem. Drugs which previously worked well are becoming ineffective. The serious falciparum strain has developed resistance to chloroquine and Maloprim in many parts of the world. Resistance to mefloquine(Lariam) is increasing.

The reasons for drug resistance are under close scrutiny. Prolonged and inappropriate use of a single drug by *local* populations encourages the malarial parasite to develop resistance to that chemical. The sensitive parasites die off and only the resistant ones multiply - survival of the fittest. Treating malaria with several drugs at once is being encouraged as it slows the development of resistance.

Some travellers are told that if tourists take 'high powered' drugs they will make drug resistance worse for the locals. *This is not true.* There is no evidence that using a particular drug for tourists promotes resistance. Tourist numbers are a 'drop in the bucket' compared to the huge local population in infected countries.

New anti-malarials are hard to find. It is a slow and expensive process. The Walter Reed Army Institute of Medical Research in Washington DC took many years to find the new drugs mefloquine and halofantrine. They screened many thousands of compounds and found *two* useful ones. This explains to some extent why new drugs are slow to appear. A new anti-malarial chemical, artemisinine is currently being used for *treatment* of malaria, not for prevention (see Cotexin p82).

Artemisinine was developed from an ancient Chinese remedy for fevers called qinghaosu (pronounced ching-how-sue). Other drugs being introduced for prevention are azithromycin, tafenoquine, and Savarine. A vaccine for malaria is still a long way off.

If you compare malaria tablets with fellow travellers you will discover recommendations vary from country to country. This is surprising since the same body of knowledge is available throughout the world.

For example: proguanil (Paludrine) is a daily malaria tablet commonly prescribed in the U.K in combination with chloroquine. Australians and New Zealanders are more likely to be given doxycyline. Travellers from the US seem more likely to be given mefloquine (Lariam). Fansidar is used in some countries for prevention of malaria. Authorities in many countries do not recommend fansidar for this purpose since it occasionally causes fatal side effects. Fansidar is safe when given for treatment of malaria, since a much lower dose is used. Amodiaquine is a malaria tablet not available in Australia but used in other countries. The *dosage* recommendations may even vary from country to country.

Comparing malaria pills is a bit like comparing blood pressure pills - everybody is on something different.

There is no correct answer.

If you were given the tablets by a reputable source, it is best to stick with the tablets that you were given. It is even more important to take them regularly.

Chopping and changing malaria tablets, on the basis of other travellers' recommendations, is very dangerous.

Local inhabitants become resistant to Malaria
People growing up in a malarious area will eventually develop *some* immunity to the parasite. The native population suffers repeated attacks throughout childhood. Those who survive into adult life have some immunity. This immunity disappears after about two years absence from the infected area. Short-term visitors have no immunity, so infections will be more severe. The locals may tell you malaria is not a problem or you don't need to take those particular tablets. *It is different for them.*

Visitors may need different tablets to the local population. Keep taking your tablets! No tablets are 100% effective, but it will be even *worse* if you don't take them properly.

Two stories about malaria

1. In 1993, a 56 year old British man and his wife went to Zimbabwe on holidays. He got sick three days after returning to the UK but was initially told he had the 'flu'. Five days later, he was admitted to hospital. Blood films showed a huge number of P. falciparum malaria parasites in his blood. Treatment was given but it was too late and he died. (His wife also became critically ill with P. falciparum but thankfully she recovered.) The couple had taken a tablet called pyrimethamine for prophylaxis on advice from friends in South Africa. This sad case is an example of why travellers should *not* take the advice of unqualified friends. Furthermore, despite all the publicity that malaria gets, people with malaria still get misdiagnosed as suffering from the flu. If you get a fever you <u>must</u> have a blood test to check for malaria, so you can be treated before complications set in.

2. A 43 year old British woman went on holiday to Ghana with her Ghanian husband. She took chloroquine and proguanil (Paludrine) for malaria prevention but did not continue taking them after she got home. She got sick two days after returning to the UK. She was admitted to an Intensive Care Unit seven days later but she died within 48 hours. This story emphasises the importance of *finishing* the course of malaria tablets after you get home.

Deaths from malaria are thankfully rare but they provide a good lesson. Make sure it does not happen to you!

MENINGITIS

Meningitis means infection of the brain and spinal cord. Meningitis is caught like the common cold - from droplets in the air - it is difficult to 'be careful' and avoid it. There are different types of meningitis with the most common ones being bacterial and viral. Bacterial meningitis is a fierce and rapid disease. The symptoms are headache, fever and drowsiness, which progresses to coma and death. If not treated it can be fatal within 48 hours. When travelling it can sometimes take a while to get to medical care.

The vaccines ('Menomune' or 'Mencevax ACWY') only protect against the 'meningococcus' bacteria of types A, C, W and Y. It will not protect against group B, viral or fungal meningitis. Vaccination is useful for parts of the world where these particular A, C, W, and Y commonly occur. It is strongly recommended that all travellers to these areas be vaccinated at least 2 weeks before leaving home.

PLAGUE

Plague is famous for causing major epidemics including the 'Black Death' in the fourteenth century when it killed about 25 million people. Worldwide there are usually 30-200 deaths reported per year. A relatively tiny outbreak (less than 100 deaths) was reported in India in 1994. There will no doubt be more epidemics in the future.

Humans contract *bubonic* plague from the bite of a rat flea. The usual symptoms of bubonic plague are fever, headache, muscular aches, shaking chills, and pain in the groin or armpit. Symptoms develop about 2-7 days after exposure. Later a bubo (swollen lymph node) develops. If the infection spreads to the lungs, the bacteria (*Yersinia pestis*) can be coughed out to infect the next person - this is known as *pneumonic* plague. Thankfully, this highly contagious type is very rare. If diagnosed early, plague is readily cured with antibiotics e.g. streptomycin, tetracycline. Plague is especially rare in travellers. Vaccination is available but not very effective. The best defence is to avoid fleas (via use of repellents) and avoid rodents (rats, rabbits, squirrels etc).

PNEUMONIA

Pneumonia is caused by a germ infecting the lungs. There are many different germs which cause pneumonia. The pneumonia vaccine (Pneumovax) is about 80% effective against the Pneumococcus. Pneumonia is more common in people over 65 years of age. Travellers may be more prone to pneumonia when travelling for the same reasons as described in the previous section about the Flu.

POLIO

Poliomyelitis is a viral disease which attacks the nerve cells of the body leading to paralysis. Usually this paralysis affects the limbs in children. In adults it can be more serious and cause death through its effect on the respiratory or breathing muscles. The disease is present worldwide. In some areas of the world up to 1% of children have some degree of paralysis due to polio. The global initiative to eradicate poliomyelitis by end of the year 2000 is the largest international disease control effort ever. The goal is to eliminate this disease from the face of the planet. Remarkable progress has been made since the initiative began in 1988. The number of polio cases has decreased from an estimated more than 350,000 cases in 1988 to just over 7,000 reported cases in 1999.

In Australia and New Zealand, Polio has been wiped out. There have been no cases in the Americas since 1991. Polio is still particularly prevalent in India, Bangladesh, Pakistan, Ethiopia, and Nigeria.

The virus is caught from food or water, and sometimes from droplets in the air (like the common cold). There is no cure, but the disease can be prevented by the oral polio vaccine (Sabin). The original course is usually given in childhood. A booster dose of the pink syrup is required every ten years to maintain immunity. Sabin is usually recommended for those travelling in developing countries. Sabin is a live vaccine. Vaccine induced Polio is a very rare complication which occurs roughly once in every 2.5 million doses distributed, usually in those whose immune system is not working or who are getting the vaccine for the first time. Ipol is a 'dead' polio vaccine which is now available for those who cannot have the live vaccine for some reason.

RABIES

Rabies is a viral disease caught from infected animals especially dogs, but also cats, monkeys, bats, wolves, and others. The animal may look normal. When the infected animal bites a person, the animal's saliva (containing the rabies virus) is injected into the wound. Rabies has an incubation period of anything from a week to over a year. Most cases develop within a month of the animal bite. Some cases take six years or more to develop.

The first symptoms of rabies are itching and burning at the site of the bite. As the disease progresses, the sufferer may develop fever, headache, agitation, fear of water and go into a coma. The virus slowly attacks the brain leading to death. Once symptoms have developed there is no known cure.

Rabies vaccination is recommended *before* departure if you are planning trips into infected areas remote from medical care. (The US authorities recommend rabies vaccine if spending more than 30 days in an infected area.)

In the event of a bite, vaccination before travel gives you more time to reach help and you need fewer needles after a bite. We do not know how long it is safe to delay vaccination. The safest course is to receive vaccination ASAP and especially within 48 hours. Rabies immunoglobulin (RI) is necessary *as well as* rabies vaccine for those persons who are bitten and have never been vaccinated. RI can be difficult to get in some developing countries. Absolutely correct treatment of all animal bites is vitally important as the following case history demonstrates.

An 11 year old boy from a middle class Thai family was bitten by his dog, which had been vaccinated against rabies twice in the preceding 2 years. He received a single puncture wound on the index finger. The wound was cleaned properly, and in accordance with the 1984 WHO recommendations, the dog was observed for unusual behaviour. The dog was found dead on the morning of the fifth day after the bite. On testing, the dog was found positive for rabies. Treatment was started immediately. The boy received the rabies vaccine correctly and some RI was injected into his arm but none into the wound. He developed symptoms of rabies on day 18 and died on day 23. Immediate vaccination and correct use of RI would probably have saved this little boy's life.

Rabies occurs in the areas outlined on the map. Reliable data on rabies is scarce in many parts of the world. The number of deaths caused each year by rabies is estimated to be 40,000 to 70,000 worldwide. India alone accounts for an estimated 20,000 of these deaths. 10 million people are estimated to receive post-exposure treatments each year after being exposed to rabies suspect animals.

Rabies Map

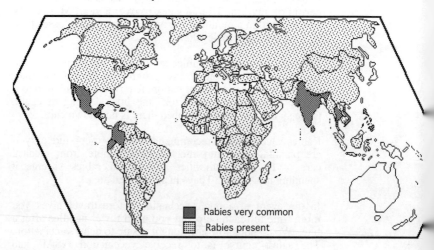

Rabies very common
Rabies present

RIVER BLINDNESS

What is it?
'River Blindness' or Onchocerciasis is a parasitic disease occurring in rural areas of Africa (including Kenya, Tanzania, Malawi) and Central America. Blindness develops after many years of infection.

How do you catch it?
The bite of a female blackfly injects the parasite under the skin. River blindness is rare in travellers, but those travelling off the beaten track should take precautions. Blackflies live near fast flowing rivers.

How do you avoid River Blindness?
There is no vaccine or preventative drugs. Avoid known infected areas. Wear protective clothing and use insect repellent liberally.

SCHISTOSOMIASIS

The following map outlines where Schistosomiasis occurs. The disease is also known as bilharzia or snail fever. The disease is present in 74 developing countries, and is estimated to infect more than 200 million people – mostly in rural areas.

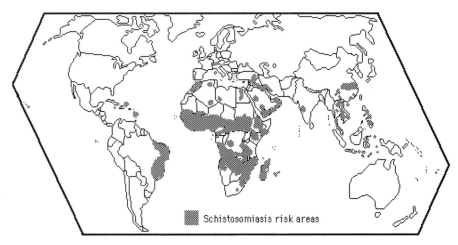

Schistosomiasis risk areas

Over the last few years, the number of tourists returning to Australia with this disease has increased dramatically. It is best to try and avoid contact with fresh water in these countries.

What is Schistosomiasis (bilharzia)?

Schistosomiasis is a disease caused by a trematode (flatworm). There are five main strains which occur in different parts of the world. Worm eggs are deposited in fresh water by infected people using lakes etc as their toilet. The worm must enter a particular snail for the first part of its life cycle. This snail lives only in slow moving, fresh water such as ponds, rice paddies or lakes. (We do not have the necessary snails in Australia.) After a time, the parasite leaves the snail and enters the water, to wait for a passing human. These creatures enter the human body by penetrating *intact* skin. They migrate through the lungs and mature in the liver, then take up residence in the blood vessels near the bladder, bowels or genitals. The worm may live for 10 years. Gradually its presence leads to scarring and organ damage.

How do you catch it?

You catch it from contact with infected fresh water. The likelihood of infection depends on where you go and how much time you are in the water. The two most popular spots where Australian travellers have picked it up are Lake Malawi, (especially around Cape Maclear) and Lake Kariba in Zimbabwe. For example in 1994 a rugby team travelled from Brisbane to Zimbabwe for about 3 weeks. Their trip included 3 days on a houseboat on Lake Kariba. Seven weeks after return two players developed their first symptoms, and of those that could be contacted 13/27 (53%) had picked up the worm. Most were not even aware of it.

What are the symptoms?

There may be temporary itching, or a rash may develop at the site of entry of the creature. The next symptoms of fever, chills, tiredness, headache, stomach problems and diarrhoea may start two weeks later, or be delayed for months. This is known as 'Katayama Fever' and occurs when the worms have matured and egg production begins. These symptoms usually last one to two weeks and then go away. They may recur a few weeks later. Some of those infected do not get any symptoms at all. As the disease progresses, visible blood may appear in the urine. Most travellers are lightly infected and unlikely to develop severe problems. Very, very rarely worms may 'get lost' and leave their eggs in the wrong place such as the spinal cord.

Diagnosis and treatment

The disease is detected by tests on urine, bowel motions or blood. The blood test may take 3-6 months after exposure to become positive. A single day's treatment with a special antibiotic praziquantel (Biltricide) will kill the adult worms. If not treated early, however, although the worms will be dead, the scarring they cause cannot be reversed.

How do you avoid Schistosomiasis?

In infected areas it is recommended you avoid contact with fresh water as described on page 55.

In practice this advice is remarkably hard to follow. For example many overland trips stay at Lake Malawi for a week. Lake Malawi is very beautiful, and very hot, and everyone else seems to swim. Scuba diving is popular. The shower water is, in most cases drawn straight from the lake (so would be just as infected as if swimming).

Many travellers report that despite their best intentions before departure, when the time comes, it is "unavoidable", "too hard to resist", or "not practical" to stay out of the water. The consequences of infection for *most* people, are not disabling. So it does become a rather philosophical question. (If one was going to worry about everything, one would probably not get out of bed in the morning – or so the saying goes.)

If fresh water contact is unavoidable, make sure you see a doctor if you get sick and have a checkup three months after exposure.

SLEEPING SICKNESS

What is it?

Sleeping sickness is an African disease caused by a parasite (trypanosome) which infects the brain leading to sleepiness and coma.

How do you catch it?

Sleeping sickness is transmitted by the bite of large flies called tsetse flies. Both sexes of tsetse flies take blood meals. These flies live in game parks and the countryside outside cities. They are active during the day and attracted to large moving objects such as cars and even horses. People on foot are less likely to be bitten. There are two types of Sleeping sickness. In West / Central Africa the tsetse fly mostly feeds on local humans beside streams and rivers. In East Africa the fly mostly feeds on cattle, near scrub and woodland.

Tsetse fly has a painful bite

Not only is there a risk of sleeping sickness, but the bite is quite painful and can penetrate clothing!

How do you avoid sleeping sickness?

There is no vaccine. There are no safe drugs for prevention. The best prevention is to avoid being bitten. You should avoid known infected areas. Insect repellent containing 'DEET' is somewhat effective but not completely. If travelling through infected areas keep the windows closed while driving, and kill any flies that enter.

See a doctor if..

You should seek medical attention if you notice a 'boil-like' swelling five or more days after a fly bite, especially if you develop fevers some time later. Most people can be cured in the early stages of infection by taking special antibiotics.

TETANUS

Tetanus (also known as Lockjaw) is a painful and serious disease. It is caused by a bacteria which enters the body through a wound. Even a tiny scratch can lead to Tetanus, though it is more common in burns, and deep or infected wounds. The bacteria grow in dead tissue and release a muscle poison, which causes all of the muscles of the body to go into terrible spasms. Tetanus can be fatal. At the very least, it requires treatment in intensive care. You can be protected from this disease by vaccination. The initial course of vaccinations is three injections in childhood. Tetanus is one of the parts of the 'Triple Antigen', (the other two are diphtheria and whooping cough). After the initial series of vaccines, one booster injection is needed every five to ten years if travelling overseas. If a wound is very likely to be contaminated by Tetanus germs, vaccination may be given more frequently.

TUBERCULOSIS

Tuberculosis (TB) is increasing worldwide, however the risk for most travellers is very low. TB risk is greatest for long-term travellers who will be working with refugees or giving health care to local inhabitants. Children of expatriate workers are at greater risk due to their contact with native children. TB is relatively hard to catch, and about 90% of those who *are* infected, remain free of symptoms for life. Persons who have TB dormant in their lungs and contract the AIDS virus will usually develop symptoms of TB. AIDS weakens the immune system and has been likened to letting the genie (TB) out of the bottle.

Before your trip, you may be recommended to have a TB test (Mantoux test or Heaf test). This is a skin test on the forearm which determines if you have been exposed to the TB germ at some time in your life. TB testing is often carried out by the local State Health Department. You need to attend the clinic *twice.* Once to have the test and again 2-3 days later to have the test read. They may also give you a chest Xray. Depending on the result, your age, and where you are visiting, you may be recommended to have a BCG (TB vaccine).

The products used in the Mantoux and BCG are live (but harmless). Because of this *live* property, certain things can interfere with their effectiveness. In the four weeks prior to the test, and the four weeks after the BCG, you cannot have:

1. Other live vaccines (except for typhoid pills as these are not absorbed into your system.). If you have the BCG and need Polio (Sabin) vaccine, these should ideally be given either on the same day or one month apart.
2. Viral infections
3. Oral Corticosteroid drugs

BCG is most effective at preventing overwhelming TB infection in children e.g. meningitis or septicemia. Generally the BCG vaccine is not given to those above 30 years of age, as its effectiveness is not well proven in that age group, though there are exceptions. Even if you do not have the vaccine, it is important to document your pre-travel TB test result. If you develop symptoms after you return home, a pre-travel TB test can be useful to help diagnose your illness.

TYPHOID

The typhoid germ causes tiredness, fever, stomach pains and a rash. Sometimes it leads to bleeding from the intestine, and rupture of the bowel. The disease lasts about three weeks, but may relapse two weeks after an apparent cure.

Typhoid has the ability to lie dormant for years in the gall bladder. Typhoid Mary felt well, yet transmitted typhoid to those around her. Typhoid is caused by a Salmonella bacteria that you can pick up from contaminated food or water - even ice.

It occurs most commonly in developing countries (especially India), where sanitation is less than ideal. Antibiotics are available to treat typhoid but prevention is better than cure.

Typhim Vi is the name of the newer typhoid vaccine. This is given as one injection only. It is recommended instead of the earlier typhoid vaccine which has now been discontinued. The earlier vaccine had more side effects, and required two injections rather than one.

The oral typhoid vaccine (Typh Vax Oral) is popular with travellers who do not like needles. It is important to avoid antibiotics and some antimalarial tablets for 1 week before, during, and for 1 week after the capsules. There are live (but harmless) organisms inside the capsules, teaching your immune system to fight typhoid. Antibiotics kill them and you will not be fully protected.

The capsules must be taken on an empty stomach, as food in the stomach will interfere with their effectiveness. The capsules need to be stored in the fridge, because heat will kill them. In the USA the recommendations for Typh Vax Oral are to take 4 capsules Day 1,3,5 *and* 7. This is reported to last 5 years (rather than one year from 3 capsules). This method is used for longer trips. If your oral typhoid vaccine is 'out of date' you need the course of capsules again, not just one booster capsule.

YELLOW FEVER

Yellow Fever is caused by a virus and spread to humans by the bite of an infected mosquito. The virus causes sudden onset of fever, four days after the bite. Most cases are mild, last less than a week, and the person makes a full recovery. Sometimes it is more serious. The liver may be damaged leading to jaundice - a yellowish tinge to the skin. (Hence the name 'Yellow' Fever.) It may cause joint pain and vomiting. Eventually the clotting system fails and bleeding occurs from the nose, gums, stomach and skin. Up to ten percent of sufferers will die.

Once upon a time, Yellow Fever was one of the great plagues of the world. There are still periodic outbreaks. In South America in 1995 there were 515 cases reported with 213 deaths. In Africa in 1995 there were 459 cases reported and 34 deaths. A total of 21,661 cases of yellow fever were reported from Africa during 1986 to 1995.

However, research has shown Yellow Fever is a greatly under-reported disease, and have estimated the true incidence to be more like ten times these figures.

A vaccination certificate may be required to enter an infected country or when leaving an infected country and entering the next (non-infected) country. In many cases officials only check the little yellow vaccination books if there is an outbreak in progress.

Yellow Fever vaccine is required for the countries outlined on the following map.

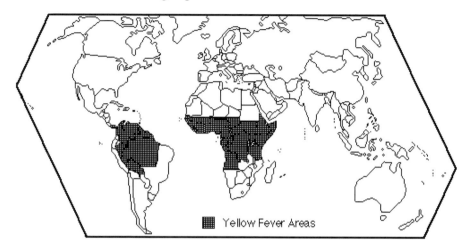

The Yellow Fever vaccine is very effective in preventing the disease. The certificate is valid 10 days after the injection, and lasts for 10 years. The vaccine is manufactured in chicken embryos, so is not recommended if you are allergic to eggs. (If you can eat eggs in minute quantities in cooking, you can be vaccinated safely.) After vaccination, you need to remain at the clinic for half an hour in case you have a serious allergic reaction (anaphylaxis). This reaction is rare (about one in a million). It can be easily treated at the clinic, but is not so easy to treat if it happens while you are driving home.

Yellow Fever vaccine is a *live* virus vaccine, so it must be given either the same day or one month before or after other live virus vaccines (e.g. polio) or they will not be as effective. Yellow Fever vaccine and Cholera vaccine (injection not oral one) should be given three weeks apart. If this is not possible, the next best thing is to have them together on the same day. Cholera vaccine suppresses the immune system and the Yellow Fever vaccine may not be effective. Yellow fever vaccination is not recommended for babies under one year of age, in pregnant women or in those who have problems with their immune system e.g. AIDS sufferers or those on cancer chemotherapy.

WHEN YOU GET HOME

Keep taking your malaria tablets for the recommended time

Post-travel checkup if necessary

Any unusual symptoms need to be reviewed by an experienced doctor as soon as possible. Tropical diseases and parasitic infestations are best treated early.

For example, you need a post-travel checkup if you are suffering any of the following: fevers, persistent diarrhoea, stomach pains, dark coloured urine, skin rashes or lumps, persistent cough, headaches or joint pains. If you have any of these on your return, or within the first three months of your return, you need a post travel checkup. You may need a pathology lab to examine your bowel motions if you still have diarrhoea. Sometimes the germ will not show up in the first pathology test and you need more tests over several days.

Fevers

If you develop a feverish illness within *two years* of your return from a malarious country, don't forget to tell the doctor where you have been.

Schistosomiasis test

If you were exposed to water that may have been contaminated with Schistosomiasis (Bilharzia) you need a checkup, *even if you feel perfectly well.* This usually means a blood test undertaken three months after your last exposure. Sometimes the test may need to be repeated six months after exposure.

Sexually Transmitted Diseases checkup

If you had sexual contacts with other travellers, locals or sex workers while you were away, you definitely need a checkup on return. Using condoms is no guarantee against contracting a sexually transmitted disease. Some diseases (like AIDS) cannot be diagnosed immediately on return, and you will need blood tests three months after exposure and sometimes later. While you are waiting for the results of the AIDS tests, it is essential you practice safe sex and notify your sexual partners of the possibility of your infection.

Worming

If you have been eating in developing countries you should probably take a course of mebendazole (Vermox) on your return; one tablet morning and night for three days. If you are suffering diarrhoea you need an examination of your bowel motions before you take these tablets.

Don't be *deterred* by all these terrible hazards...
Just be *careful.*

Ode to a world traveller

Travellers come in many types
But one thing is the same
Getting sick while you're away
Would be an awful shame

To be a healthy traveller
Means following the rules
Casting caution to the winds
Is only for the fools

Have your shots before you go
To keep you out of harm
Some vaccines are oral
So do not hurt your arm

In amongst your baggage
Take a first aid kit:
Drugs to deal with problems
If and when they hit

Beware of too much luggage
Gear will weigh you down
You do not want to strain your back
Lugging it through town

If you don't want memories
Revolving round the loo
And suffering from travellers trots,
Then this is what you do

Remember that you cannot eat
Exactly when you wish
The germs may be invisible
And waiting in your dish

Avoid those foods that are not cooked
Both recently and well
Or several hours later
Your guts may feel like hell

Don't drink water from the tap
Above all don't add ice
But you can add some iodine
To make the water nice

Or pour yourself a can of coke
Or something that is sealed
Or masticate upon some fruit
That you yourself have peeled

If up into the mountains
Sometime you wish to go
The golden rule to keep in mind:
Ascending must be slow

If you should find a lover
Sometime while you're away
Don't forget about safe sex
Cos AIDS is here to stay

If you're hot in Africa
And you're going swimming
Don't forget that in some lakes
Bilharzia is brimming

If you get close to puppy dogs
And if you get a bite
A rapid course of rabies shots
Will help to set you right

Don't let mossies bite you
All through the night or day
Using Rid and Bed nets
Will keep those bugs away

If you get a fever
And malaria is rife
Quickly have a blood test
Or you may lose your life

If you plan a hire car
Wear your seat belt tight
It is also safer
Not to drive at night

Keep away from motor bikes
The traffic will be tough
If you fall off and hurt yourself
The hospitals are rough

Be careful when you cross the street
Do not make that dash
A truck may come from nowhere
And squash you in a flash

Now I've told you all of this
My advice is done
Go and have a healthy trip
But most of all have fun!

INDEX

A

Accidents 47, 69
Acetazolamide 65, 116
Acupuncture 51
ADT 10
Aeroplane safety 50
AIDS
  a few details 125
  prevention 51
Alcohol
  after vaccinations 14
  and AIDS 51
  and altitude 65
  and flying 38
  and road accidents 49
  and Scuba diving 69
  and spas 68
  germicidal properties 42
  overseas brews 52
  treating hangovers 104
  with malaria tablets 19
Aldecin 94
Allergies 94
Altitude sickness 64
Alum 44
Aminopyrine 28
Amoebic dysentery 90
Amoxil 116
Amoxycillin 94, 116
Antihistamine 116
Antiseptic hand wash 25
Arab countries 61
Aralen 117
Arm bands 70
Artemisinin 82, 136
Asthma 30
Athlete's foot 103
Atovoquone 120
Avil 116
Avlochlor 117
Avomine 122

B

Bactrim 116
  for diarrhoea 89, 92
  for kidney infection 111
Balconies 48
Balustrades 48
Bathrooms 48
BCG 11, 145
Beconase 94
Bed bugs, 53
Bee stings treatment 100
Bepanthen 25
Beta Blockers 21
Biaxsig 123
Bilharzia 55, 141, 149
Biltricide 122, 143
Bites 100
Black Death 138
Black Fever 132
Blackfly 141
Bladder infection 111
Bleeding
  nose 95
  wounds 95
Blockout 23
Blood pressure 56
Blood transfusion 28
Boiling water 44
Bubonic Plague 138
Burns treatment 99
Buscopan 88, 116
Bushman 16
Butazolidin 28

C

Caffeine 57
Calliente 48
Cars 49
Cephalexin 117
Chagas' disease 53, 125
Chancroid 51
Chaud 48
Chickenpox vaccine 9, 10

Children
  before you go 32
  fluoride 29
  if they get sick 115
  medical supplies 26
  poisoning 27
  preventing illness 63
Chinchona 133
Chloramphenicol 28, 117
Chlorine to purify water 44
Chloromycetin 107, 117
Chloroquine 18, 20, 82, 117
  malaria prevention 18
  side effects 20
  malaria treatment 82
Chlorquin 117
Cholera
  about the disease 126
  certificate validity 9
  vaccine 11
Ciguatera 126
Cipro 117
Ciprofloxacin 89, 117
Ciproxin 117
Citravescent 110
Claratyne 116
Clarification 44
Cleaning teeth 44
Clioquinol 28
Codeine 121
Cold climates 58, 67
Cold injuries 105
Collapse 113
Coloxyl 93, 117
Constipation 93
Contraceptive 59
Cotexin 82, 136
Cruise 70
Culture Shock 72-74
Cyclospora diarrhoea 92
Cystitis 61, 111

D

Dairy products 43
Dapsone 120
Decongestants 69
DEET 16
Dehydration 58, 104

Dengue Fever 127
Dental emergencies 108
Dentures 29
Diamox 65, 117
Diarrhoea treatment 85
    post travel checkup 149
Diethyl toluamide 16
Diflucan 118
Dimenhydrinate 118
Diphenoxylate 118
Diphtheria 10,128
Diving 69
Doctors
    finding them overseas 76
    letter for drugs 27
Docusate sodium 117
Doryx 118
Doxycycline 18, 21, 94, 118
Drammamine 71,118
Driving safety 49

E

Ear first aid 107
Eating
    safely 42
    unsafely 43
Econazole 118
Embassy 76
Emergency contraception 111
Enterovioform 28
Epilepsy 30
Erythromycin 122
Euhypnos 123
Exercises on the plane 39
External cardiac compression 114
Eye first aid 106

F

Fainting 13
Fansidar 82, 118, 136
Fasigyn (Tinidazole) 92,123
Fever
    post travel check 149
    treatment 79

Finding doctors 76
Fires 48
First aid training 33
Flagyl 90, 121
Flea bites treatment 100
Fleas 53
Flopen 119
Flu 128
    Flu vaccine 8, 9
Flucloxacillin 119
Fluconazole 111, 118
Fluid balance 87
Fluoride 29
Food poisoning 83
Frostbite 105
Fungus 103
Fybogel 92

G

Gamma Globulin 11, 130
Gastrolyte 119
    for diarrhoea 86
    for vomiting 85
Gastrostop 120
Genital warts 51
Giardia 92
Gonorrhoea 51
Goretex 58

H

Hair loss 19
Halfan 82
Halofantrine 82, 135
Hangover treatment 104
Havrix (Hepatitis A vaccine)
    how vaccine is given 11
    how long vaccine lasts 9
Heaf 145
Heart disease 30
Heat
    avoiding heat stroke 56
    treating heat stroke 104

Hepatitis
  how vaccines are given 11
  A? B? C? D? E? 129 -131
  how long vaccines lasts 9
Herpes 51
Hitchhiking 62
HIV 30, 125
Hookworms 55
Hotels 48
Humidity 57
Hydrogen peroxide 96
Hygiene for women 59
Hyoscine hydrobromide 120
Hyoscine butylbromide 116
Hypothermia 105

I

Ibilex 117
Ibuprofen 119
Ice 43
Illegal drugs 52
Imigran 30
Imodium 119
  for diarrhoea 88
Influenza (Flu)128
  vaccine 8,9
Injection 11
Insect bite treatment 100
Insects 53
Insurance 28
Iodine 44,45,119

J

Japanese B Encephalitis
  about the disease 131
  how long vaccine lasts 9
  how vaccine is given 11
Jellyfish sting treatment 102
Jetlag 34, 40

K

Kala azar 132
Keflex 117
Kidney infections 111
Kitchens 46
Knee pain 66
Kwells 71, 120
KY 51

L

Lariam 18, 20, 121
  discovery 136
  malaria treatment 81
  side effects 20
Lateral Recovery Position 113
Leeches 53
Leishmaniasis 53,132
Letter for medications 27
Levlen 59
Lockjaw 144
Lomotil 88, 120
Loperamide 88, 120
Lyme Disease 53

M

Malaria
  about the disease 132-136
  life cycle of parasite 133
  map 132
  most important points 15
  parasite growth chart 134
  prevention 15-21
  tablets 18-21
  standby treatment 80-82
Malarone 18, 82, 120
Maloprim 120
Mantoux 145
Maxolon 85, 121
Mebendazole 121, 149
Medical Insurance 28
Medical Kit 23-27
Mefloquine 18,20,121

Melatonin 34
Mencevax 11
Meningitis
  about the disease 137
  how long vaccine lasts 9
  how vaccine is given 11
  vaccine strains 137
Menomune 11
Menstruation irregularity 61
Metamucil 92
Metoclopramide 121
Metronidazole 92, 121
Microgynon 59
Micropur 44
Morning after pill 111
Mosquito
  avoidance 16
  treatment of bites 100
Mosquito net
  chemical treatment 17
  how to use 16
Motion sickness 70-71
Motor bikes 48
Motor vehicle accidents 49
Mouth to mouth resuscitation 114
Mouth ulcers 21,109
Moxacin 116
Mud huts 53

N

Night driving 49
Nivaquine 117
Norfloxacin 122
  for diarrhoea 90
  for kidney infection 111
Normal temperature 79
Normison 40, 123
Noroxin 122
Nosebleed treatment 95
Nurofen 119

O

Onchocerciasis 141
Oral contraceptive 59
Ovale 134

Overheating 56
Oysters 43

P

Packing 35
Paludrine 18, 122
  side effects 21
  use in UK 136
Paracetamol 122
Parasites
  avoidance 55
  post travel check 149
Periods irregular 61
Permethrin 17
Pevaryl 61, 118
Phenergan 122
Pilots 21
Pinguecula 67
Plague 53, 138
Pneumonia 138
Polaramine 116
Polio
  about the disease 138
  how long vaccine lasts 9
  how vaccine is given 10
Post travel check-up 149
Potable Aqua 44
Praziquantel 122, 143
Pregnancy 31, 38
  and Lariam 20
  medical supplies 26
  vaccinations 8
Prescriptions 28
Pressure earache 108
Prickly heat 103
Prochlorperazine 123
Proguanil 120,122
Promethazine 71,122
Pseudoephedrine 123
Puritabs 44
Pyrimethamine 118, 120, 137

Q

Quinine 82,123

R

Rabies background 139
  prevention 54
  pre bite vaccination 11
  how long vaccine lasts 9
  treatment if you get bitten 101
  map of affected areas 140
Rash 103
Rats 138
Raw food/vegetables 43
Rehydration fluid recipe 86
Relapsing Fever 53
Resochin 117
Restaurants 46
River Blindness 141
Rohypnol 62
Roxithromycin 94, 123
Rulide 123
Runny nose 93

S

Sabin 10, 139
Safe sex 51
Salads 43
Salicylic acid 103
Salmonella 145
Salt 57
Sandfly diseases 132
Saunas 68
Schistosomiasis 141-143
  post travel checkup 149
SCOP 71, 123
Scorpions 53, 101
Scuba
  need for a medical 30
  safety hints 69
Sea sickness 70
Seafood 43
Seat belts 49
Security 62
Septrin Forte 116
Sex and disease 51
Side effects
  all drugs 78
  vaccinations 13

Sightseeing hazards 47
Silver to purify water 44
Simplotan 122
Sinus 93
Skin rash 103
Sleeping on planes 38
Sleeping sickness 143
Smoking
  and air travel 38
  and altitude 65
Snakes 101
Sneezing 93, 94
Snow blindness 66, 106
Snow mobiles 68
Snow skiing 67
Sofradex 107
Soframycin 106
SoloSite gel 98
Spas 68
Spiders 53
Stamaril 11, 14, 147
Stemetil 85,123
Stoppers 88
Storage of drugs 27
Street stalls 46
Sudafed 69, 108, 123
Suitcase 35
Sulphadoxine 118
Sulphamethoxazole 116
Sunbathing 57
Sunburn
  and altitude 66
  treatment 100

Symptoms

altitude sickness 64
athletes foot 103
behaviour change 64, 105
bites
  insect 100
  snake/dog etc 101
blood
  in diarrhoea 89
  in urine 111
burns 99
chills 79
cold fingers/toes 105
confusion 106

constipation 93
cough
    dry 94
    green sputum 94
    pink frothy sputum 64
cramps in stomach 86
diarrhoea 85-92
discharges
    ear 107
    eyes 106
    vaginal 111
dizziness 105
eye problems 106
fever 79
flu like 81
frostbite 105
fungal rash 103
gums sore 109
hangover 104
headache 64
hypothermia 106
insomnia 64
itch
    skin 103
    vaginal 111
jellyfish sting 102
loss apetite 90
malaria 81
motion sickness 70
mouth ulcers 21,109
nausea 64, 70, 105
pain
    back 111
    eyes 106
    fingers/toes 105
    gum 109
    headache 79
    muscles 81, 110
    on urination 110
prickly heat 103
sea sickness 70
shortness of breath 64
skin damage 94
skin rash 103
sprains 110
sunburn 100
sweating 105
swelling
    at altitude 66
    on aeroplanes 38
temperature 79

thrush 111
tick removal 101
tingling limbs 65,105,126
urine burning 110
ulcers
    mouth 21,109
    skin/tropical 95
vaginal itch 111
vision loss 106
vomiting 85
weight loss 90
wind 90
wounds 95
Syphilis 51

T

TB 144
Teeth 29,108
Teldane 94, 116
Temazepam 122
Temperature 79
Tetanus
    about the disease 144
    about the vaccine 9, 10, 13
The Pill 59
Thrush 61, 110, 111
Ticks 53, 100
Tinadermuse 103
Tinea 103
Tiniba 123
Tinidazole 92,123
Toboggans 68
Travel insurance 28
Trekking
    fitness training 33
    pre-departure medical 30
Trimethoprim 111, 116
Tropical Ear 107
Tsetse flies 143
Tuberculosis 144
Tuberculosis test 11
Typh Vax Oral 146
Typhim Vi 146
Typhoid the disease 145
    how long vaccine lasts 9
    side effects of vaccine 14
Typhus 53

U

Ulcers
  mouth 109
  tropical 95
Ural 110
Urine infection
  prevention 61
  treatment 110

V

Vaccination 8
  how long they last 9
  schedule 12
  side effects 13
  which ones? 8
Vaqta (Hepatitis A vaccine)
  how vaccine is given 11
  how long vaccine lasts 9
Varilrix (chickenpox vaccine)
  how vaccine is given 10
  how long vaccine lasts 9
Vermox 121, 149
Vibramycin 118
Vitamin B
  mosquito avoidance 16
Vitamin C powder 45
Vivax malaria 134
Vomiting 85

W

Wasp sting treatment 100
Wetstuff 51
Women's medical supplies 26
Women 59-61
  pregnant traveller 31
  travelling in arab countries 61
Worms
  prevention 55
  treatment 149
Wound care checklist 95-99

Y

Yellow Fever
  about the disease 146-7
  how long vaccine lasts 9
  how vaccine is given 11
  side effects of vaccine 13-14

Entertain and inform your audience

Guaranteed!

Would your audience enjoy something different and unforgettable?

Does your conference, meeting or seminar need a presentation that is unique, interesting, and relevant to almost every participant?

Dr Deborah Mills is a leading specialist in the field of travel health, and has full professional ASM accreditation with The National Speakers Association of Australia. Her wealth of clinical experience in travel medicine practice combined with many great stories gives you have a public speaker who is informed, entertaining, and good for your health.

All presentations are fully customised to your specific requirements and the interests of your audience.

What participants have said

"Dr Deb - funny, interesting, stimulating, informative"

...Excellent. ...Superior. ...Very interesting. ...Extensive knowledge of topic. ...Great slides. ...Easy to understand. ...Language was clear and not too technical. ..She didn't rush so gave me time to comprehend. ...10/10 ...Lively. ...Friendly and professional. ...Out of the ordinary!

"Loved Dr Deb - she was brilliant"

Call her now on 0408 199 166 or 61 7 3221 9066 and start planning to surprise and delight your audience.

For more information, check out
http://www.travellingwell.com.au